Praise for
Everything Belongs

"Rohr at his finest: insightful cultural critique woven with strong connection to both the marginalized and the contemplative. This small book brings prayer and solitude together with the wounds of the world in insightful synthesis." — *The Other Side*

"Rohr gets to the heart of Christianity and what it means to be contemplative. It is the sort of book one could recommend (or give) to someone who is searching for something 'more.'" — *Monos*

"Simply written yet deeply challenging. . . . At the base of all reality, Rohr writes, is God's 'radical grace.'"
— *The Mennonite*

"Rohr steers the reader toward a deeper prayer life. With the novice in mind, Rohr helps the reader know what contemplation is all about and how one is to get out of the way in the quest." — *St. Anthony Messenger*

"The challenge of this book is simple, yet profound: 'Be aware.' Be aware of God in all things."
— *Catholic Library World*

Everything
Belongs

Also by Richard Rohr

Called, Formed, Sent, with Thomas C. Welch, 2002

The Enneagram: A Christian Perspective, with Andreas Ebert, 2001

Hope Against Darkness: The Transforming Vision of St. Francis of Assisi in an Age of Anxiety, with John Bookser Feister, 2001

The Good News According to Luke: Spiritual Reflections, 1997

Jesus' Plan for a New World: The Sermon on the Mount, with John Bookser Feister, 1996

Job and the Mystery of Suffering: Spiritual Reflections, 1996

Enneagram II: Advancing Spiritual Discernment, 1995

Radical Grace: Daily Meditations, 1995

Quest for the Grail, 1994

Near Occasions of Grace, 1993

Experiencing the Enneagram, with Andreas Ebert et al., 1992

The Wild Man's Journey: Reflections on Male Spirituality, revised edition (with Joseph Martos), 1992, 1996

Simplicity: The Art of Living, 1991

Discovering the Enneagram: An Ancient Tool for a New Spiritual Journey, with Andreas Ebert, 1990

Why Be Catholic?: Understanding our Experience and Tradition, with Joseph Martos, 1989

The Great Themes of Scripture: New Testament, with Joseph Martos, 1988

The Great Themes of Scripture: Old Testament, with Joseph Martos, 1987

Everything Belongs

The Gift of
Contemplative Prayer

REVISED AND UPDATED
EDITION

Richard Rohr

A Crossroad Book
The Crossroad Publishing Company
New York

The Crossroad Publishing Company
481 Eighth Avenue, New York, NY 10001

Printed in the United States of America

The text font is 10.75/15 ITC Stone Informal.
The display fonts are Codex and Univers Condensed.

Library of Congress Cataloging-in-Publication Data

Rohr, Richard.
    Everything belongs : the gift of contemplative prayer / Richard
Rohr.– Rev. and updated ed.
        p.   cm.
    ISBN 0-8245-1995-7 (alk. paper)
    1. Contemplation. 2. Spiritual life –Catholic Church.   I. Title.
BV5091.C7R64 2003
248.3′4 –dc21

                                                         2003001248

        4   5   6   7   8   9   10   10   09   08   07   06   05

I want not only to thank
but to dedicate this book to
Clink Thomson.
His years of friendship, advice,
support, and endless patience
have sent my taped words all over the world.
Now he is foolish enough to do
what they say never to do:
put it down in writing.
With his humor and my seriousness,
we make a tolerable team.

One always learns one's mystery
at the price of one's innocence.

Pulling out the chair
Beneath your mind
And watching you fall upon God —
There is nothing else for Hafiz to do
That is any fun in this world!

—Shams-ud-din Mohammed Hafiz,
Muslim mystic (1320–89)

Contents

Inherent Unmarketability

How do you make attractive that which is not?

How do you sell emptiness, vulnerability, and nonsuccess?

How do you talk descent when everything is about ascent?

How can you possibly market letting-go in a capitalist culture?

How do you present Jesus to a Promethean mind?

How do you talk about dying to a church trying to appear perfect?

This is not going to work
(admitting this might be my first step).

one

Center and Circumference

Turning and turning in the widening gyre
The falcon cannot hear the falconer;
Things fall apart; the center cannot hold;
Mere anarchy is loosed upon the world,
The blood-dimmed tide is loosed, and everywhere
The ceremony of innocence is drowned;
The best lack all conviction, while the worst
Are full of passionate intensity.

—William Butler Yeats, "The Second Coming"

We are a circumference people, with little access to the center. We live on the boundaries of our own lives "in the widening gyre," confusing edges with essence, too quickly claiming the superficial as substance. As Yeats predicted, things have fallen apart and the center does not seem to be holding.

If the circumferences of our lives were evil, it would be easier to moralize about them. But boundaries and

edges are not bad as much as they are passing, accidental, sometimes illusory, and too often in need of defense
or "decoration." Our "skin" is not bad; it's just not our
soul or spirit. But skin might also be the only available
beginning point for many contemporary people. Earlier
peoples, who didn't have as many escapes and means to
avoid reality, had to find Essence earlier —just to survive.
On the contrary, we can remain on the circumferences
of our lives for quite a long time. So long, that it starts
feeling like the only "life" available.

Not many people are telling us there is anything more
to life. I am told that the primary mediating institutions
in our deconstructed society are the media and the business world. While these institutions are not bad, they are
inadequate to name our soul or entice our spirit. We are
at a serious disadvantage if we take them as "the bottom
line" of our existence, which is ironically exactly what we
call the business or economic perspective.

Let's presume that there was an earlier age when
people had easy and natural access to their souls and
openness to transcendent Spirit. I am not sure that this
age ever perfectly existed, any more than the Garden
of Eden, where all was naked and in harmony, but if it
did, it consisted of people who were either loved very
well at their center or who suffered very much around
the edges —probably both. The path of prayer and love
and the path of suffering seem to be the two Great

Paths of transformation. Suffering seems to get our attention; love and prayer seem to get our heart and our
passion.

But most of us return to the garden by a more arduous
route. In his poem *Four quartets,* T. S. Eliot called it the
path of "observance, discipline, thought and action. The
hint half guessed, the gift half understood." This ordinary path *back* to Paradise is the blood, guts, and ecstasy
of the whole biblical text: usually three steps forward and
two steps backward, just like our lives.

The ordinary path is a gradual awakening and an
occasional quieting, a passion for and a surrendering
to, a caring and a not caring at all. It is both center and
circumference, and I am finally not in control of either
one. But we must begin somewhere. For most of us the
beginning point is at the edges. This reality, felt and not
denied, suffered and enjoyed, becomes the royal road to
the center. In other words, reality itself, our reality, my
limited and sometimes misinterpreted experience, still
becomes the revelatory place for God. For some reason
we seem to prefer fabricated realities to the strong and
sensitizing face of *what is.*

Yet the great teachers tell us not to stay on the circumferences too long or we will never know ourselves or
God. The two knowings, in fact, seem to move forward
together. This movement might also be understood as
conversion, transformation, or growth in holiness. You

cannot make this journey in your head, alone. Actually, you cannot make it alone at all. You must be led.

Less than a block from where I used to live in downtown Albuquerque there is a sidewalk where the homeless often sit against the wall to catch the winter sun. Once I saw a fresh graffiti chalked clearly on the pavement. It touched me so profoundly that I immediately went home and wrote it in my journal. It said, "I watch how foolishly man guards his nothing — thereby keeping us out. Truly, God is hated here." I can only imagine what kind of life experience enabled this person to write in such a cutting but truthful way. I understood anew why Jesus seemed to think that the expelled ones had a head start in understanding his message. Usually they have been expelled from what was unreal anyway — the imperial systems of culture, which demand "in" people and "out" people, victors and victims. In God's reign "everything belongs," even the broken and poor parts. Until we have admitted this in our own soul, we will usually perpetuate expelling systems in the outer world of politics and class. Dualistic thinking begins in the soul and moves to the mind and eventually moves to the streets. True prayer, however, nips the lie in the bud. It is usually experienced as tears, surrender, or forgiveness.

Perhaps I can presume that this homeless person is not formally educated in theology or psychotherapy; yet through the path of suffering, and maybe prayer, this person is in touch with both essence and edges — and knows who God is. This is why St. Bonaventure and others said that a poor uneducated person might well know and love God more than a great theologian or ecclesiastic. You do not resolve the God question in your head — or even in the perfection of moral response. It is resolved *in you,* when you agree *to bear the mystery of God:* God's suffering for the world and God's ecstasy in the world. Agreeing to this task is much harder, I'm afraid, than just trying to be "good."

Living in this consumer-driven world, we are often infected by what some call "affluenza," a toxic and blinding disease which makes it even more difficult for us to break through to the center. Our skin-encapsulated egos are the only self that most of us know, and this is where we usually get trapped. It is fair to say that the traps of mind and ideology are as toxic and as blinding as the so-called "hot sins" of drunkards and prostitutes, though they are harder to recognize. Most of us have to be taught how to see; true seeing is the heart of spirituality today.

Journey to the Core

How do we find what is supposedly already there? Why isn't it obvious? Why should we need to awaken our deepest and most profound selves? And how do we do it? By praying and meditating? By more silence, solitude, and sacraments? Yes to all of the above, but the most important way is to *live and fully accept our reality.* This solution sounds so simple and innocuous that most of us fabricate all kinds of religious trappings to avoid taking up our own inglorious, mundane, and ever-present cross.

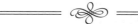

We do not find our own center; it finds us. Our own mind will not be able to figure it out.

For some reason, it is easier to attend church services than quite simply to reverence the real — the "practice of the presence of God," as some have called it. Making this commitment doesn't demand a lot of dogmatic wrangling or managerial support, just vigilance, desire, and willingness to begin again and again. Living and accepting our own reality will not feel very spiritual. It will feel like we are on the edges rather than dealing with the essence. Thus most run toward more esoteric and dramatic postures instead of *bearing the mystery of God's suffering and joy inside themselves.* But the edges of our lives — fully experienced, suffered, and enjoyed — lead us back to the center and the essence.

The street person feels cold and rejected and has to go to a deeper place for warmth and truth. The hero pushes against his own self-interested ambition and eventually discovers that it does not matter very much anyway. The alcoholic woman recognizes how she has hurt her family and breaks through to a Compassion that is much bigger than she is. In each case, the edges that we call reality have suffered, informed, and partially self-destructed. Then they often show themselves to be unnecessary or even part of the problem. Only then do we recognize and let go of the boundaries and edges surrounding our soul. No wonder that the saints and mystics so often use those unpopular words of "surrender" and "suffering." As Jesus says, "Unless the grain of wheat dies, it remains just a grain of wheat" (John 12:24).

We do not find our own center; it finds us. Our own mind will not be able to figure it out. We collapse back into the Truth only when we are naked and free —which is probably not very often. *We do not think ourselves into new ways of living. We live ourselves into new ways of thinking.* In other words, our journeys around and through our realities, or "circumferences," lead us to *the core reality,* where we meet both our truest self and our truest God. We do not really know what it means to be human unless we know God. And, in turn, we do not really know God except through our own broken and rejoicing humanity. In Jesus, God tells us that God is not different from humanity. Thus Jesus' most common and almost exclusive self-name is "The Human One," or "Son

of Humanity." He uses the term seventy-nine times in
the four Gospels. Jesus' reality, his cross, is to say a free
"yes" to what his humanity finally asks of him. It seems
that we Christians have been worshiping Jesus' journey
instead of *doing* his journey. The first feels very religious;
the second just feels human, and not glorious at all.

We tend not to see the transformative pattern of death
and rebirth, and how God is our transformer, until *after*
the fact. In other words, we are slow learners, and that
is why most spiritual teachers are found in the second
half of their lives. For example, Julian of Norwich, the
holy English anchoress (1342–1416), had an amazing
ability to move beyond either-or thinking. She could live
with paradox, unanswered questions, immense inner
conflicts, and theological contradictions — and still trust
and be at peace. One wonders if this was the fruit of
her womanhood, her nonacademic status, her at least
twenty years of solitude in the anchorhold, or just the
fruit of one night's "showing," as she called it. Certainly
she represented the best of what we mean by "contemplative seeing." As she put it, "First there is the fall, and
then there is the recovery from the fall. But *both* are the
mercy of God." Maybe you can't believe that until the
second half of life.

How did we ever lose that kind of wisdom? Especially
when it is almost everybody's experience? Only the spacious, contemplative mind can see so broadly and trust

so deeply. The small calculating mind wants either/or, win or lose, good *or* bad. Yet we all know that the deacon sings of *felix culpa* on Holy Saturday night. We were saved, the liturgy says, by a "happy mistake." Jesus reminded Julian that his crucifixion was the worst thing that happened in human history and God made the best out of it to take away all of our excuses. As they were for Jesus, "our wounds become honors." The great and merciful surprise is that we come to God not by doing it right but by doing it wrong!

Calmly Held Boundaries

On a very practical level, the problem is that contemporary Westerners have a very fragile sense of their identity, much less an identity that can rest in union and relationship with God. Objectively, of course, we are already in union with God, but it is very hard for people to believe and experience this when they have no strong sense of identity, no boundaries, and no authentic religious experience. People who have no experienced core are trying to create identities and let go of boundaries. For them, it might be helpful to explain that prayer in the early stages is quite simply a profound experience of that core: of who we are, as Paul says, "hidden with Christ in God" (Col. 3:3).

Those who rush to artificially manufacture their own identity often end up with hardened and overly defended edges. They are easily offended and are always ready to create a new identity when the current one lets them down. They might become racists or control freaks, people who are always afraid of the "other." Often they become codependent or counterdependent, in either case living only in reaction to someone or something else. To them, negative identity is created quickly and feels sort of like life. Thus many people, even religious folks, settle for lives of "holier than thou" or lives consumed by hatred of their enemies. Being over and against is a lot easier than being in love.

Many others give up their boundaries before they have them, always seeking their identity in another group, experience, possession, or person. Beliefs like, "She will make me happy," or "He will take away my loneliness," or "This group will make me feel like I belong" become a substitute for doing the hard work of growing up. It is much easier to belong to a group than it is to know that you belong to God. Those who firm up their own edges and identity too quickly without finding their center in God and in themselves will normally be the enemies of ecumenism, forgiveness, vulnerability, and basic human dialogue. Their identity is too insecure to allow any movement in or out and their "Christ" tends to be very small, tribal, and "just like them." If your prayer is not enticing you outside your comfort zones, if your Christ is not an occasional "threat," you probably need to do some growing up and learning to love. You have to develop an ego before you can let go of it. Maybe that is why Jesus just *lived* thirty years before he started talking. Too often, young adults full of Yeats's "passionate intensity" about doctrine and dogma and which group is going to heaven use God to shore up their nonselves. Such traditionalism is actually avoiding the Tradition of transformation through death and rebirth.

Others let go of their edges too easily in the name of being tolerant and open-minded, but even here "discernment of spirits" is necessary. There is a tolerance in true contemplatives because they have experienced the One Absolute, their own finite minds, and the passing character of all things. This is the virtue of humility or maybe even patience. But there is another tolerance today which is simply a refusal to stand up for anything. To this kind of tolerant person, there are no boundaries worth protecting. The tolerance of the skeptic is largely meaningless, creates little that lasts, and is unfortunately characteristic of much progressive and humanistic thought today.

Traveling the road of healthy religion and true contemplation will lead to calmly held boundaries, which need neither to be defended constantly nor abdicated in the name of "friendship." This road is a "narrow road that few travel upon" these days (Matt. 7:14). It is what many of us like to call "the Third Way": the *tertium quid* that emerges only when you hold the tension of opposites.

The gift that true contemplatives offer to themselves and society is that they know themselves as a part of a much larger Story, a much larger Self. In that sense, centered people are profoundly conservative, knowing that they stand on the shoulders of their ancestors and the Perennial Tradition. Yet true contemplatives are paradoxically risk-takers and reformists, precisely because they have no private agendas, jobs, or securities to maintain. Their security and identity are founded in God, not in being right, being paid by a church, or looking for promotion in people's eyes. These people alone can move beyond self-interest and fear to do God's necessary work. Look at out how many saints, theologians, and especially woman foundresses of orders were corrected, threatened, and even persecuted by the church during their lifetimes. God is always bigger than the boxes we build for God, so we should not waste too much time protecting the boxes.

People who have learned to live from their center in God know which boundaries are worth maintaining and which can be surrendered, although it is this very struggle that often constitutes their deepest "dark nights." Both maintaining and surrendering boundaries ironically require an "obedience," because they require listening to a Voice beyond their own. If you want a litmus test for people who are living out of one's True Self, that might be it: they are always *free to obey,* but they might also *disobey* the expectations of church and state to obey who-they-are-in-God. Think of St. Paul, Thomas à Becket, Joan of Arc, Thomas Merton, or Dorothy Day. Scary stuff, this contemplation!

God is always bigger than the boxes we build for God, so we should not waste too much time protecting the boxes.

By contrast, probably the most obvious indication of noncentered ("ec-centric") people is that they are, frankly, very difficult to live with. Every one of their ego-boundaries must be defended, negotiated, or worshiped: their reputation, their needs, their nation, their security, their religion, even their ball team. They convince themselves that these boundaries are all they have to worry about because they are the sum-total of their identity. You can tell if you have placed a lot of your eggs in these flimsy baskets if you are hurt or offended a lot. You can hardly hurt saints because they are living at the center and do not need to protect the circumference of feelings and needs. Ec-centric persons though, are a hurt waiting to happen. In fact, they will create tragedies to make themselves feel alive. I am told that personnel work now represents 80 percent of the time and energy that American companies have to expend. You might even say that a certain degree of contemplative seeing is actually necessary for the effective life of an institution or a community.

Toward the end of his life, Carl Jung said that he was not aware of a single one of his patients in the second half of life whose problems could not have been solved by contact with what he called "the Numinous" and we would call God (*Letters,* 1973, 1:377). An extraordinary statement from a man who had no great love for institutional religion. I believe that we have no real access to *who we really are* except in God. Only when we rest in God can we find the safety, the spaciousness, and the scary freedom to be *who* we are, *all* that we are, *more* than we are, and *less* than we are. Only when we live and see through God can "everything belong." All other systems exclude, expel, punish, and protect to find identity for their members in ideological perfection or some kind of "purity." The contaminating element always has to be searched out and scolded. Apart from taking up so much useless time and energy, this effort keeps us from the one and only task of love and union. As the Hasidic masters taught their students, "Rake the muck this way. Rake the muck that way. It will still be muck. In the time you are brooding, you could be stringing pearls for the delight of heaven."

I hope this book helps you to string some good pearls together — and not to waste too much time brooding.

two

Vision of Enchantment

Love people even in their sin, for that is the semblance of Divine Love and is the highest love on earth. Love all of God's creation, the whole and every grain of sand of it. Love every leaf, every ray of God's light. Love the animals, love the plants, love everything. If you love everything, you will perceive the divine mystery in things. Once you perceive it, you will begin to comprehend it better every day. And you will come at last to love the whole world with an all-embracing love.

—Fyodor Dostoyevsky, *The Brothers Karamazov*

Let me begin with hope. I hope our understanding of prayer is coming to a greater simplicity. If prayer isn't simple by the time you finish reading this, I will have failed. We must keep in mind, however, that the purpose of the exploration of prayer is not to get anywhere. We Western people are goal-oriented consumers, and we can't imagine doing anything that won't get us some-thing. But with full deliberation, we need to understand our exploration is not an effort to get anywhere.

My starting point is that we're already there. We can-not attain the presence of God because we're already totally in the presence of God. What's absent is aware-ness. Little do we realize that God is maintaining us in existence with every breath we take. As we take another it means that God is choosing us now and now and now. We have nothing to attain or even learn. We do, however, need to unlearn some things.

All religious teachers have recognized that
we human beings do not naturally see; we
have to be taught how to see.

To become aware of God's presence in our lives, we have to accept what is often difficult, particularly for people in what appears to be a successful culture. We have to accept that human culture is in a mass hypnotic trance. We're sleep-walkers. All religious teachers have recognized that we human beings do not naturally see; we have to be taught how to see. That's what religion is for. That's why the Buddha and Jesus say with one voice, "Be awake." Jesus talks about "staying watchful"

(Matt. 25:13, Luke 12:37, Mark 13:33–37), and "Buddha" means "I am awake" in Sanskrit. Jesus says further, "If your eye is healthy, your whole body is full of light" (Luke 11:34).

Thus, we have to learn to see what is there. Such a simple directive is hard for us to understand. We want to attain some concrete information or achieve an improved morality or learn some behavior that will make us into superior beings. But there's no question here of meritocracy. Although we have a "merit badge" mentality, prayer shows us that we are actually "punished" by any expectation of merit and reward. For that expectation keeps us from the truly transformative experience called grace. We worship success. We quaintly believe we get what we deserve, what we work hard for and what we are worthy of. It is hard for Western people to think any other way than in these categories.

Experiencing radical grace is like living in another world. It's not a world in which I labor to get God to notice me and like me. It's not a world in which I strive for spiritual success. It's not a cosmic game of crime and punishment. Unfortunately, a large percentage of the world's religions do teach that, if usually indirectly. Religious people are afraid of gratuity. Instead, we want God for the sake of social order, and we want religion for the sake of social controls.

I'd like to say something a bit different about prayer, and therefore about religion. Prayer is not primarily saying words or thinking thoughts. It is, rather, a stance. It's a way of living *in* the Presence, living in *awareness* of the Presence, and even of enjoying the Presence. The full contemplative is not just aware of the Presence, but trusts, allows, and delights in it.

All spiritual disciplines have one purpose: to get rid of illusions so we can be present. These disciplines exist so that we can see what is, see who we are, and see what is happening. On the contrary, our mass cultural trance is like scales over our eyes. We see only with the material eye.

If we are to believe Jesus, nothing is more dangerous than people who presume they already see. *God can most easily be lost by being thought found.* Chapter 9 of John's Gospel, containing the story of the man born blind, illustrates this concept beautifully.

The story begins with a simple brilliant statement. Jesus *sees* the man born blind. The observation is brilliant because it so simply captures what Jesus does. He is a seer. The disciples immediately ask him, "Now, who has sinned because this man was born blind, his parents or himself?" But Jesus dismisses the entire argument and moves it to another level sacramentally. He uses mud to anoint the man's eyes, and the blindness is healed. The

rest of the chapter chronicles "good" people who fight
Jesus for doing this.

The Pharisees argue that Jesus cannot be from God so
the healing cannot have really happened — even though
it is clear it did. It's right in front of them. They ignore
this evidence and make a logical and theological argument: a sinner can't work miracles and Jesus hasn't
observed the Sabbath so he's a sinner. In the final para-
graph they accuse the man himself of being a sinner.
They see sin everywhere except in themselves. "You, a
sinner through and through, who are you to tell us?"
The man is shrewd enough not to get into theological
debate. He sticks to his story. "All I know is that I was
blind and now I see."

Jesus ends this wonderful illumination story with a
final devastating line (v. 39): "It is for judgment that I
have come into the world. So those without sight may see
and those with sight be turned blind." Hearing this, the
Pharisees say, "We are not blind, surely." (We're orthodox, we're good Christians, we're clergy!) Jesus replies,
"Blind? If you were, you would not be guilty. But since
you say, 'We see,' your guilt remains" (9:41).

Cultivating the Beginner's Mind

Jesus calls us to exactly what the Zen master calls his students to. I once stayed in a Zen monastery in Japan. The

master was calling monks who had been there for years to what they called "beginner's mind." Similarly, one of Jesus' favorite visual aids is a child. Every time the disciples get into head games, he puts a child in front of them. He says the only people who can recognize and be ready for what he's talking about are the ones who come with the mind and heart of a child. It's the same reality as the beginner's mind. The older we get, the more we've been betrayed and hurt and disappointed, the more barriers we put up to beginner's mind. We must never presume that we see. We must always be ready to see anew. But it's so hard to go back, to be vulnerable, to say to your soul, "I don't know anything."

Try to say that: "I don't know anything." We used to call it *tabula rasa* in Latin. Maybe you could think of yourself as an erased blackboard, ready to be written on. For by and large, what blocks spiritual teaching is the assumption that we already know, or that we don't need to know. We have to pray for the grace of beginner's mind. We need to say with the blind man, "I want to see."

Spirituality is about seeing. It's not about earning or achieving. It's about relationship rather than results or requirements. Once you see, the rest follows. You don't need to push the river, because you are in it. The life is lived within us, and we learn how to say yes to that life. If we exist on a level where we can see how "everything belongs," we can we trust the flow and trust the life, the life so large and deep and spacious that it even includes its opposite, death. We must do this, because it is the only life available to us, as Paul wrote to the Colossians, "You have died [the small ego self], and the life you now have is hidden with Christ in God [the Godself]. When Christ is revealed — *and he is your life* — you too will be revealed in all your glory with him" (Col. 3:3–4).

Religion has tended to create people who think they have God in their pockets, people with quick, easy, glib answers.

Jesus calls us beyond this cultural hypnotic trance, beyond sleepwalking, by his countercultural actions. It's like the awakening clap of the Zen master's hand. He says we are trapped, we can't see. He tries by every means he can, often by way of parable, to subvert the normal way of seeing. Parables turn reality upside down. When I was at the Zen temple, I was sitting with the monks in that lotus position (which I can't do). After about five minutes, a gong rang and they all, even the older monks, jumped up and rushed out of the room. I wondered if it was a fire drill! Nobody had warned me. I felt stupid; I didn't know the script. I said to myself, "I'll just sit here so I don't look any more stupid than I feel already."

Now the room was completely deserted and there I was, sitting on my little pillow. In pain. After about fifteen minutes, the monks reentered, one after another, took their seats, and we still had to sit another half hour. When we could talk later, I asked what had happened. They told me, "We should have warned you; this is the day we get our *koan*." A *koan* is a little impossible paradoxical riddle that one can't resolve by normal means of logic. If we use our calculating, educated, highly literate minds, we'll sit there forever. There's no way out or through. The master told me that sometimes he has to give the same *koan* to the same monk for two or three years before he can move past it. He was giving out *koans* that day. One has to let go of the usual logical thought patterns and move to a broader, more contemplative mind to solve the riddles. Their function is to get them beyond their certitudes and ego-securities, to return them to a childlike openness, so that they can be taught again and let go of their present comfort zone. This is exactly what Jesus is saying in chapter 9 of John's Gospel. "Because you say, 'we see,' you are blind."

Religion has lost sight of Jesus' message here. It has not tended to create seekers or searchers, has not tended to create honest humble people who trust that God is always beyond them. We aren't focused on the great mystery. Rather religion has tended to create people who think they have God in their pockets, people with quick, easy, glib answers. That's why so much of the West is understandably abandoning religion. People know the great mystery cannot be that simple and facile. If the great mystery is indeed the Great Mystery, it will lead us into paradox, into darkness, and into journeys that never cease. That is what prayer is about.

Transformative Images

I looked at some of the images and parables of Jesus. So many of them are subversive and so many of them are about seeing. They are really his form of *koan*.

For example, four are about things that are *lost or hidden*. Why so many about things lost or hidden unless the message is about seeing? Things appear to be lost that aren't obvious at first glance: the treasure hidden in the field (Matt. 13:44), the yeast hidden in flour (Matt. 13:33), the lost coin (Luke 15:8), and the lost sheep (Matt. 18:12). When things are lost, we are required to go on a search. We must admit that what we are looking for is not obvious. We have to want to see it, and we have to learn how to see.

Another set of parables that is about *growth from very small beginnings*. There is the familiar mustard seed, of course (Matt. 13:31). In chapter 4 of Mark, he describes the growth from seed to shoot to ear to grain (4:26–29). The mystery of that growth develops over time, just as we only learn how to see slowly. Matthew speaks of hidden leaven and invisible salt.

Then there is the sower parable itself in Mark 4:1–9. It was this passage that inspired me to start taping my talks in 1972. Back then audio tapes weren't used for talking. We had just got out of the radio stage. Why would anyone want to tape a talk? Music made sense, but no one would listen to someone talk! But Sr. Pat Brockman, O.S.U., had the wild idea of taping the talks I was then giving to teenagers. Behind every man there is a woman, urging him on. She said she'd go down and talk St. Anthony Messenger into it. I said I really didn't think it would work. (I didn't want to hurt her feelings.) She said, "Well, just promise me this. You'll pray for a day and we'll meet at this time tomorrow and we'll ask God for an answer. (Those were our charismatic days when we played Bible roulette!) I agreed, even though it seemed awfully presumptuous. Why would I presume anything I'd have to say would be taped? Who would buy the tapes? But I agreed to meet the next day. We'd open the scriptures and whatever we saw I'd accept as the will of God. I put my finger down, and while Pat watched anxiously, I looked at the passage. It said, "The sower went out to sow the seed" (Mark 4:3). Well, that sounded like making tapes to us. So we did, and I haven't stopped since.

The parable says the seed fell on several different types of soil. Some just aren't ready for the Word. They're not there yet. It's not their fault; when the student is ready the teacher will arrive. Normally we let God in the way we let everything else in. We meet God at our present level of relational maturity: preoccupied, closed, stuck, or ready. Most spiritual work is readying the student. Both soil and soul have to be a bit unsettled and loosened up a bit. As long as we're too comfortable, too opinionated, too sure we have the whole truth, we're just rock and thorns. Anybody throwing us seed is just wasting time.

I encountered the minds of many "readied beginners" on my 1994 preaching tour in Japan and the Philippines. The person who set up the tour said, "Richard, in Japan, Christians are only one-third of 1 percent of the population. I can't promise you big crowds. There might be only twenty or twenty-five people there, but they are like trumpets. They haven't heard ten thousand sermons like Americans, for whom this would be just one more and who would then continue with business as usual. They will remember much of what you say, word for word, and it will go out to a hundred other people. They are that desirous of spirituality." Sure enough. People from my first tour in 1981 came up to me and quoted what I had said back then, word for word. Now that's fertile soil. Word for word! They changed their lives! And they were back for more thirteen years later. That's a teachable person, a real "disciple."

In our culture, we suffer from, among other things, a glut of words, a glut of experiences, and, yes, a glut of tapes, books, and ideas. When we have too many words, we tend not to value them, even if they might contain life for us. We find it hard to be a disciple with a beginner's mind because we've heard it all before, from many directions. We can't absorb it all. I am told that if you imagine the amount of information available to the ordinary person as one unit at the time of Jesus, it took until the year 1500 for that to double. Soon after the invention of the printing press, it doubled every hundred years, then every fifty, then, in this century, every ten years. At the end of the second millennium it doubled every seven months. We are all on overload and understandably confused and conflicted. This prompts many to move "over and out" into dogmatism, skepticism, or psychic numbness. We desperately need some disciplines to help us know *how* to see and what is *worth* seeing, and what we *don't need* to see. My hope is that you may be the last kind of soil that Jesus speaks of as "producing thirty, sixty, even a hundredfold" (Mark 4:8).

For example, we had a wonderful staff assistant here a few years ago, Don Kaliski. Talk about beginner's mind! After every retreat here at the center, we'd ask him how it went. He'd always say, "It changed my life!" And in

him it was true. He'd take it in and decide to live in a
new way. Somehow he was able to maintain a beginner's
mind and start over at every retreat.

To maintain a beginner's mind while surrounded by
distracting information, we need the gift of spiritual discernment. The fifth chapter of Matthew talks about the
law not being dismissed "until its purpose is achieved"
(5:18). The point is not to obey the law as much as to find
the purpose of the law. What is it for? In the West people
don't understand spiritual discernment. We get moral-
istic about the law as an end in itself. But the law does
not give life; only the Spirit gives life, as Paul details in
Romans and Galatians. When Jesus teaches the law, it's
for the sake of its purpose being achieved. It is never an
end in itself, as he makes very clear when he defends his
disciples who were picking grain on the Sabbath (Luke
6:1–5).

Adopting a beginner's mind also requires that we be
willing to respond and change because we are aware of
our own mixture of good and evil. Jesus uses a number
of *mixture images* that illustrate this tension. They seem
to say this world is a mixture of different things, and
unless you learn how to see, you don't know to separate;
you get lost in the weeds and can't see the wheat (Matt.
13:24–30). When a student comes and says, "Should I
pull out the weeds?" Jesus says, "No." He says to let them
both grow together until the harvest (Matt. 13:29). Then,

at the end of time, he will decide what is wheat and what is weed. This idea has had little effect on Western moral theology. But we are a mixture of weed and wheat and we always will be. As Luther put it, *simul justus et peccator*. His whole tradition said we are simultaneously saint and sinner. That's the mystery of holding weed and wheat together in our one field of life. It takes a lot more patience, compassion, forgiveness, and love than aiming for some illusory perfection that is usually blind to its own faults. The only true perfection available to us is the honest acceptance of our imperfection.

If we must have perfection to be happy with ourselves, we have only two choices. We can either blind ourselves to our own evil (and deny the weeds) or we can give up in discouragement (and deny the wheat). But if we put aside perfection and face the tension of having both, then we can hear the good news with open hearts. It takes uncommon humility to carry the dark side of things. It takes a kind of courage to carry the good side, too. Archetypically, "the crucified one" always hangs between these two thieves —paying the price within himself just as we must do. (See Luke 23:32–34; note Jesus forgives *both* thieves.)

Another mixture image is of yeast and flour (Matt. 13:33). The salt is still another (Matt. 5:13). In the thirteenth chapter of Matthew, he says, "This is what a scribe of the kingdom is like." Scholars think he is describing himself. He continues, "He throws out the dragnet and pulls in things both old and new." In other words, he preserves the best of what we call conservative and the best of what we call progressive. This is always a rare vocation, because it pleases hardly anybody, especially our own ego need to have the "whole truth."

Jesus' *illumination images* approach the problem of arriving at a beginner's mind in a different way. The lamp images in Mark 4:21 and Luke 8:16 seem to speak of nondenial and conversation that moves beyond group-speak or political correctness. Your personal seeing is to be public illumination: "put the lamp on a lampstand." Jesus loves the image of the lamp and calls the entire Christian people a lamp on a mountaintop (Matt. 5:15). We should be an illuminated and honest people who have learned how to see reality in depth, capable of recognizing self-serving "truths" and cultural lies. He hopes to create a wisdom culture. In Matthew 25 Jesus describes the bridesmaids as people who have their lamps lit. They are ready to illuminate the darkness and bring clarity and meaning, not just group lies or ideology disguised as religion. As we will see, the path of prayer seems to be the only light through this darkness. Without it, most of us will sell out to group pressure and group-think (more than ever in this media-controlled culture, where there is little "media literacy").

Ultimately, all Jesus' parables are of the kingdom. The kingdom he describes is an alternative to sleepwalking. He points to a way of seeing beyond cultural hypnosis. We have to really hear a parable or a *koan* so our false and ordinary view of reality is undermined, or at least relativized and called into question. The parables of the kingdom are almost always subversive with regard to conventional thinking and so-called common sense.

The Sign of Jonah

Beginner's mind is a posture of eagerness, of spiritual hunger. The beginner's mind knows it needs something. This is a rare feeling in today's treacherously seductive culture, however. Because it is so immediately satisfying, it is hard to remain spiritually hungry. We give answers too quickly, take away pain too easily, and too quickly stimulate. We are at a symbolic disadvantage as a wealthy culture. Jesus said that the rich man or woman will find it hard to understand what he is talking about. The rich can satisfy their loneliness and longing in false ways, in quick fixes that avoid the necessary learning. In terms of soul work, *we dare not get rid of the pain before we have learned what it has to teach us.* That's why the poor have a head start. They can't resort to an instant fix to any problem: aspirin, a trip, or some entertainment. They remain empty whether they want to or not.

To resist the instant fix and acknowledge oneself as a beginner is to be open to transformation. Children, Jesus' models, are eager to grow up. They know they will be transformed, and they eagerly await it. I think Jesus' primary metaphor for the mystery of transformation is the sign of Jonah (Matt. 16:4, 12:39, Luke 11:29). This sign has taken on a great significance for me. In Luke's Gospel passage in which Jesus tells us, "It is an evil and adulterous generation that wants a sign" (Luke 11:29), he then says the only sign he will give us is the sign of Jonah. As a good Jew, Jesus knew the graphic story of Jonah the prophet, who was running from God and was used by God almost in spite of himself. Jonah was swallowed by the whale and taken where he would rather not go. This was Jesus' metaphor for death and rebirth. Think of all the other signs, apparitions, and miracles that religion looks for and seeks and even tries to create. But Jesus says it is an evil and adulterous generation that looks for these things. That's a pretty hard saying. He says instead we must go inside the belly of the whale for a while. Then and only then will we be spit upon a new shore and understand our call. That's the only pattern Jesus promises us. Paul spoke of "reproducing the pattern" of his death and thus understanding resurrection (Phil. 3:11). That teaching will never fail. The soul is always freed and formed in such wisdom. Native religions speak of winter and summer; mystical authors speak of darkness and light; Eastern religion speaks of yin and yang or the Tao. Seasons transform the year; light and darkness transform the day. Christians call it the paschal mystery, but we are all pointing to the same necessity of both descent and ascent.

The paschal mystery is *the* pattern of transformation. We are transformed through death and rising, probably many times. There seems to be no other cauldron of growth and transformation.

We must go inside the belly of the whale for a while. Then and only then will we be spit upon a new shore and understand our call.

We seldom go freely into the belly of the beast. Unless we face a major disaster like the death of a friend or spouse or loss of a marriage or job, we usually will not go there. As a culture, we have to be taught the language of descent. That is the great language of religion. It teaches us to enter willingly, trustingly into the dark periods of life. These dark periods are good teachers. Religious energy is in the dark questions, seldom in the answers. Answers are the way out, but that is not what we are here for. But when we look at the questions, we look for the opening to transformation. Fixing something doesn't usually transform us. We try to change events in order to avoid changing ourselves. We must learn to stay with the pain of life, without answers, without conclusions, and some days without meaning. That is the path, the perilous dark path of true prayer.

Simone Weil said, "It is grace that forms the void inside of us and it is grace alone that can fill the void." Grace leads us to the state of emptiness, to that momentary sense of meaningless in which we ask, "What is it all for? I don't want to wake up tomorrow." A woman whose husband had just died called me yesterday. She could not imagine why she would want to live and couldn't imagine how it would ever be different again. All I could do was just tell her, "Believe me, believe me." She said, "I'll trust you." I told her, "Some day this immense bottomless pit of pain will go away."

It should be the work of Christians who believe in the paschal mystery to help people when they are being led into the darkness and the void. The believer has to tell those in pain that this is not forever; there is a light and you will see it. This *isn't* all there is. Trust. Don't try to rush through it; we can't leap over our grief work. Nor can we skip over our despair work. We have to feel it. That means that in our life we will have some blue days or dark days. Historic cultures saw grief as a time of incubation, transformation, and necessary hibernation. Yet this sacred space is the very space we avoid. When we avoid darkness, we avoid tension, spiritual creativity, and finally transformation. We avoid God, who works in the darkness — where *we* are not in control! Maybe that is the secret: relinquishing control.

Liminality and Transformation

Let me introduce you to a concept anthropologists call "liminality." It's also called liminal space. The Latin word *limen* means threshold. It is central to initiation rites and is a good metaphor for preparation for transformation. We discuss it frequently in our men's retreats. We find ourselves in a strange position in the West. We alone, of all the centuries of civilization, culture, and tribe, do not have initiation rites for the young, especially for young men.

Other cultures have recognized that people in general, and boys in particular, are not born; they are made. These cultures took it upon themselves to transform a boy into a man. Certain things had to be told him because he would not come to them naturally. The boy would naturally want to ascend, and religion had to teach him the language of descent. He had to learn the way of tears and how to learn to let go.

These initiation rites are always about leading the boy out of the world of business as usual (the cultural trance we sleepwalk in) and leading him into liminal space. It's a voluntary displacement for the sake of transformation of consciousness, perspective, and heart. People didn't assume that just by getting up every day they would learn what they needed to know. They had to be displaced and shocked to teach them that this isn't the only world. There is another world, much bigger and more inclusive, that both relativizes and reenchants this world that we take as normative.

If we bring to a retreat all the baggage and mentality of business as usual, we aren't really making a "retreat." So nothing new or transformative can happen. I've given lots of retreats. Certain people come to hear what they already know. If I say something they don't know, I can see their arms cross and they mentally pack up and leave. But if we hear only what we already know, we simply cannot learn or grow. That attitude is a sure ticket to ignorance. Alcoholics say that without humility and honesty, nothing new happens. These virtues, humility and honesty, are the foundation of all spirituality, but they are hard won. Most of us have to crawl our way back to them. Usually we don't go unless the pain of circumstance forces us. Jonah didn't dive over the edge of the boat; they threw him in!

Liminal space induces a type of inner crisis to help us make a needed transition. In brief, it should wake us up a bit. That's what is meant by a liminal experience. The two greatest liminal experiences, of course,

are birth and death. My mother's death experience was
a liminal experience for me as were two births I was privileged to attend. We can't understand such events except
through experience. Many people try not to experience
them. We use denial or drugs to prevent us from really
experiencing what is happening.

The experiences don't have to be so difficult, though.
A visit to another culture can jar us awake, if it is truly a
visit to another culture. If we go and stay in an American
hotel, eat at McDonald's, and complain because things
are not like they are in Chicago, we really haven't left
home. We've let go of nothing. We have to see that others
don't see things the way we do. We need to have our fundamental assumptions questioned. Maybe our questions
are not the only ones and maybe America is not the center of the world. Maybe our religion isn't the only way
to look at reality. Or maybe I haven't really understood
how my religion has transformed many people, as have
the other great world religions, each in its own way. Liminal space is always an experience of displacement in the
hope of a new point of view. No wonder Jesus called it
"turning around." Unfortunately, the Greek word *metanoia,* which literally means to move "beyond the mind,"
is usually translated "repentance" and no longer points
to its much deeper meaning.

Like travel, transformation is a kind of journey. A good journey starts with knowing where we are and being willing to go someplace else. How do we know we have gone someplace else? Until we have points of comparison, we don't understand much. When we have those, we can relativize our private absolute center. That's what liminal space is for: to pull us out of our private absolute center. It relativizes our experience. Sometimes a good liturgy can do this to us. I've seen lives changed by a fine liturgy. The sacraments can have an enormous power, as can a good retreat, a true "I-Thou" encounter with another person, or a failure that makes everything fall apart.

When we first fall in love, for example, we are temporarily taken out of ourselves. It doesn't last; it's infatuation. (Some say that means "false fire.") But it does give you a new perspective on reality. The world looks entirely different when we first fall in love. Rites of passage of any type, including conversion, move you from here to there. When you talk this way to people, they often shrink from the experience. They say, "I'm a Catholic (or a Protestant or a Muslim or a Jew); I don't want to learn another way to look at things." They act as though they have God all figured out. These people betray a need for control at all costs; unfortunately the cost is high indeed.

Jesus talks frequently about *metanoia:* turning around, or changing your mind. I remember having problems with that myself. I thought, "What am I supposed to turn around?" I'm baptized, I'm confirmed, I've gone to the Eucharist, and I'm even ordained! Why should I turn around? I'm right. I've got the truth and the education to prove I've got it." How foolish. That's precisely the blindness Jesus is talking about. That's why some people in high religious positions can be the blindest of all. People the most obedient to commandment and church formulas can very often be the hardest to convert. They've taken the symbol for the substance. They've taken the ritual for the reality. They've taken the means for the end and become inoculated from the experience of the real thing.

That's called idolatry, when we worship and protect the means. It actually keeps us from the journey to the end. Religions should be understood as only the fingers that point to the moon, not the moon itself. But much of institutional religion seems to give people just enough "God talk" to enable them to forever avoid any direct and frightening religious experience. A vision quest was supposed to be just that for Native Americans. They were not supposed to come back until they had seen another world. Until you've seen an alternative reality, until you've seen a larger reality and God has shown God's face, you're not initiated. Time spent in a hermitage or in any prolonged period of solitude often does this for people. In the year 1400 there were thirteen hundred Franciscan hermitages in Europe. Religious seekers said we must go apart, break our addiction to the world, and live in another way before we return to the world. Only then, they believed, could we be fully in the world but no longer trapped by it.

Beyond Our Comfort Zone

When we first have a liminal experience, it's very inflating. People are often a bit obnoxious after their "born again" experience, their baptism in the Spirit, or their first religious retreat — at least for a few days. You can't blame them. It's so exciting to finally see the truth. But if they don't have humility and honesty at that point, it's really dangerous. *They use the language of descent for an ascent.* Unfortunately, it is rather common today among all groups, especially if people have wasted many years on "drugs, sex, and rock and roll." God becomes a way for the humiliated ego to reascend.

The last experience of God is frequently the greatest obstacle to the next experience of God. We make an absolute out of it and use it to strengthen our ego, to self-aggrandize and self-congratulate. Then, of course, nothing more happens. That's why Jesus repeats the admonition to conversion. We need to be converted again and again. We aren't born again. We are born again and again and again. Accepting and acting upon that principle takes a lot of letting go. If we aren't willing to move out of our comfort zone, it won't happen. All great spirituality is about letting go.

God is patient, however. We don't have to move out of our comfort zone every day. God gives us little plateaus — breathing spaces wherein we unfortunately get ensconced again. Everything is now wrapped around us, to affirm our present status and security and identity. It gives us a momentary sense of superiority. We hold on to this false security. We need failure and quiet time to recognize this pattern. We don't want our cobweb of identity taken away. Without grace we will not enter into the void, and without grace the void will not be filled. All we can do is try to keep our hands cupped and open and ask God to teach us how to keep our hands cupped and open. The events and experiences of life teach us how.

Too often, however, we do not allow the events and experiences of life to teach us the habit of grace. What we have instead, and mass produced in our society, are what I call "liminoid" experiences. Our society has mass produced these as substitutes for liminal experiences. They look like a movement out of our cozy space, but aren't. "I have to get away from it. I'm going to the beach for two weeks," people say. When we see people come back, they're not refreshed at all. They have the same old agenda, the same old fears, the same old anger. They let go of nothing at the beach. Their way of looking hasn't changed, so neither has their agenda. Their way of feeling and responding to reality is exactly the same. Maybe they got some good sleep, and that's good for a while, but three days after the vacation they'll be just like they were before. Then they'll need another vacation.

I fear that a good deal of liturgy is liminoid. And much recreation does not re-create us, but is only diversionary. I think that's why Americans need so much recreation and entertainment. If it doesn't really entertain and refresh, we will need more very soon. But for open persons, those who know how to receive and let events teach them, a little bit goes a long way. If they see one beautiful flower they have to write a poem about it; they don't have to revisit and see it again because it is printed somewhere inside of them. We always need more if we were never *there*.

Real sexual encounter can be liminal. But if the counseling I'm doing and the relationships I have touched upon are any indication, most sexual encounters are liminoid. They avoid the great letting go, the scary intimacy, and the great breaking through. But maybe this only happens once or twice in a lifetime. Drinking and drugs and anything that lowers our consciousness do not lead to liminal experience. I'm sure alcoholics could confirm that. Alcohol and drugs do not provide an entrance into *deeper* consciousness. Instead, they *lessen* our consciousness and awareness. But great religion seeks utter awareness and full consciousness, so that we can, in fact, receive all. Everything belongs and everything can be received. We don't have to deny, dismiss, defy, or ignore. What is, is okay. *What is, is the great teacher.* I have always seen this as the deep significance of Jesus' refusal of the drugged wine on the cross (Matt. 27:34).

I write this to lead you, in some way, away from normalcy. Normalcy is the way things appear to be. "The bottom line," as businessmen love to say. They say, "I heard your talk, Father, but the bottom line is...." I know they're sincere, but they've never seen an alternate reality. "Bottom line" means only one thing: buying and selling. What a strange and unsatisfying foundation for life, for spirituality!

The Christian vision is that the world is a temple, and buying and selling in the temple is the one thing that drove Jesus to anger and violence. It destroys inherent value and replaces it with an utterly false seeing: market value, the world of meritocracy and exchange rates. It destroys the soul. It had to be driven out or there would be no temple. There is no temple if you live merely in the world of buying and selling — the so-called bottom line. In that world everything is weighed. We say, "Let's see, she gave me a gift worth $25 so I have to... no, it didn't cost that much, probably only about $16 or $17... —

that kind of talk. Who cares? That kind of thinking is a dead end. Preoccupation with exchange value and market value tends to blind us almost totally to inherent value. Prayer, though, reconnects us with inherent value. Everything becomes priceless if it is sacred. And everything is sacred if the world is a temple.

When we can see the image of God where we don't want to see the image of God, then we see with eyes not our own.

Do you think the soul is satisfied with this "buying and selling in the temple"? It will never be. Seeing the world in terms of such transactions will never satisfy the soul or feed the spirit because they mask reality. The purpose of prayer and religious seeking is to see the truth about reality, is to see *what is*. And at the bottom of *what is* is always goodness. The foundation is always love.

I don't know that I have touched it yet. At some moments, God has parted the veil and it's tasted very good. It's tasted like the real. Enlightenment is to see and touch the big mystery. The big pattern. The Big Real. Jesus called it the kingdom of God; Buddha called it enlightenment. Both Buddhists and Hindus speak of *nirvana*. Philosophers might call it Truth. Most of us just call it love. Here is a mantra you might repeat throughout your day:

God's life is living itself in me. I am aware of life living itself in me.
God's life is living itself in me. I am aware of life living itself in me.

There's no answer, no problem-solving, simply aware-ness. You cannot *not* live in the presence of God. You are totally surrounded by God as you read this. St. Patrick said,

> God beneath you,
> God in front of you,
> God behind you,
> God above you,
> God within you.

You cannot earn this God. You cannot prove yourself worthy of this God. Feeling God's presence is simply a matter of awareness. Of enjoying the now. Deepening one's presence. There are moments when it happens. Then life makes sense. Once I can see the Mystery here, and trust the Mystery even in this piece of clay that I am, in this moment of time that I am — then I can also see it in you. I am able to see the divine image in myself, in you, and eventually in all things. Finally, the seeing is one. How you see anything is how you will see everything.

Jesus pushes seeing to the social edge. Can you see the image of Christ in the *least* of your brothers and sisters? He uses that as his only description of the final judgment. Nothing about commandments, nothing about church attendance, nothing about papal infallibility: simply a matter of our ability to see. Can we see Christ in the least of our brothers and sisters? "They smell. They're a nuisance. They're on welfare. They are a drain on our tax money," we say. Can we see Christ in the people, the nobodies who can't play our game of success? When we can see the image of God where we don't want to see the image of God, then we see with eyes not our own.

Finally, Jesus says we have to love and recognize the divine image even in our enemies. He teaches what many thought a leader could never demand of his followers: love of the enemy. Logically that makes no sense. But soulfully it makes absolute sense, because in terms of the soul, it really is all or nothing. *Either we see the divine image in all created things, or we don't see it at all.* Once we see it, we're trapped. We see it once and the circle keeps moving out. If we still try to exclude some (sick people, blacks, people on welfare, gays, or whomever we've decided to hate), we're not there. We don't yet understand. If the world is a temple, then our enemies are sacred, too. The ability to respect the outsider is probably the litmus test of true seeing. It doesn't even stop with human beings and enemies and the least of the brothers and sisters. It moves to frogs and pansies and weeds. *Everything* becomes enchanting with true sight. One God, one world, one truth, one suffering, and one love. All we can do is participate.

three

Ego and Soul

"Is there anything that I can do to make myself enlightened?"

"As little as you can do to make the sun rise in the morning."

"Then of what use are the spiritual exercises you prescribe?"

"To make sure you are not asleep when the sun begins to rise."

—Zen master to his disciple

The contemplative secret is to learn to live in the now. The now is not as empty as it might appear to be or that we fear it may be. Try to realize that everything is right here, right now. When we're doing life right, it means nothing more than it is right now, because God is in this moment in a nonblaming way. When we are able to experience that, taste it and enjoy it, we don't need to hold on to it. The next moment will have its own taste and enjoyment.

Because our moments are not tasted or full or real or in the Presence, we are never full. We create artificial fullness and try to hang on to that. But there's nothing to hold on to when we begin to taste the fullness of the now. God is either in *this now* or God isn't at all. As we grow older, we tend to become control freaks. We need to control everybody and everything, moment by moment, to be happy. If the now has never been full or sufficient, we will always be grasping, even addictive or obsessive. If you're pushing yourself and others around, you have not yet found the secret of happiness. Know that things are okay as they are. This moment is as perfect as it can be. The saints called this the "sacrament of the present moment."

None of us are completely present. So don't feel guilty. This is the ideal, the enlightened moments that come now and then. But we do know that when we are manipulating, changing, controlling, and fixing, we are not there yet. The calculating mind is the opposite of the contemplative mind. The first is thought by the system, the second by the Spirit.

I use this prayer to try to draw myself and others into a contemplative frame of mind:

Be still and know that I am God.
Be still and know that I am.
Be still and know.
Be still.
Be.

To become more present, we must reach into a deep inner spaciousness; then we can speak with more intelligence and clarity, with a little less ego, and with less of our agenda in the way. I hope we can say ego is not bad. It is necessary. The only problem is that our culture teaches that ego is the only game in town. We take it a little too seriously and take the private ego as if it is full reality. The nature of the ego is that it tries to fix, name, control, and insure everything for itself. We want predictability. But that fixes us in the past. What was, is, so we are trapped in repeating it and nothing new happens.

The religious version of egocentricity is wanting to be right and wanting to be in control. To give that up is major surgery. Religion might call it major conversion: as Jesus says, "Unless the grain of wheat dies, it remains just a grain of wheat" (John 12:24). There is a small "I" that has to let go so that the true "I" can be born. What can't happen if we live entirely within the small "I" is, quite simply, love. Love is almost not possible there. The small "I" only knows itself by comparison, by image, by how we look. As long as we are comparing and differentiating from the other, we can't love the other. We judge it. As soon as we are in a judging mode (higher/lower, superior/inferior), we can't love. The small "I" does not permit a realm of freedom where love flourishes. What flourishes is control, comparison, and competition —which blind us to love.

If producing and consuming are the only games we play, they harden into our reality. Yes, it is a false reality, but it can grow more real to us as we grow older. It's consequently harder to convert as we grow older. If we still believe that the system of producing and consuming is the real world, the only world, by the time we're fifty, there's almost no way out. It requires a major transformation of consciousness to learn how to let go of this false reality if we've lived a life of comparing, differentiating, judging, and controlling. Win/lose is the only game most of us understand. We have a constant unspoken need for domination and actually find no enjoyment in win/win situations. Love and freedom cannot grow in such self-preoccupied and calculating minds. When we live out of ego, we impose our demands on reality. But when we live in God's presence, we await reality's demands on us.

The great spiritual teachers are not concerned about domination and power in the sense our culture uses it.

Their power is in descent, not ascent. I find my deepest power is what Jesus visualizes on the cross as power-lessness. We Christians believe that the crucifixion of Christ — seemingly a moment of utter powerlessness — is actually his moment of greatest power. This recognition is at the core of all spiritual teaching. It is a recognition that dramatically turns one's reality upside down. But with contemplation, this paradox eventually moves from being a dilemma to becoming a choice.

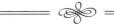

The present moment has no competition; it is not judged in comparison to any other.

If we are not tasting the fullness of the now, we will play the games of power to fill the emptiness. If we're playing the domination game, we can be as trapped on the left as on the right. Our great disillusionment with so much of even contemporary progressive thinking is that it is still playing the power game. It's playing it on the left side, the liberal side, but the game's the same. Even while being politically correct, we are still looking for control and righteousness. That demon has not yet been exorcised. Freshness and creativity will not come from there. Such false "enlightenment" is either all in the head or is mere counterdependency on that which it opposes.

Jesus' notion of the kingdom of God will not come from political correctness because it is the same game on the other side of the playing field. The ego has just found another way to be right: with vegetarianism, for example! I'm not against vegetarianism, but if it's used as our new way to be in control and morally superior, we are not enlightened. While crunching organic carrots, some assure their egos bite by bite, "I am right." Health can become the new name of salvation. I suppose the religion of health is as close as a materialist culture can come to salvation. We start with a preoccupation with the body, so physical health is as close as we can come to a full life. I'm all for health, but dieting, exercising, health food, and elaborate spas can be just a materialist definition of salvation. You can usually tell if your pursuit of health is an ego control game if it becomes obsessive and is not balanced with the work of mind, heart, spirit, and soul. How can we be fully present to another human being if all we see is their eating habits so we can judge them accordingly?

The present moment has no competition; it is not judged in comparison to any other. It has never happened before and will not happen again. But when I'm in competition, I'm not in love. I can't get to love because I'm looking for a new way to dominate. The way we know this mind is *not* the truth is that *God does not deal with us like this.* The mystics, those who really pray, know this. Those who enter deeply into the great mystery do not experience a God who compares, differentiates, and judges. They experience an all-embracing receptor, a receiver who looks at the divine image in us and almost refuses to look at the contrary. Julian of Norwich, who is my favorite mystic teacher, says, for example, "The Lord looks on his servants with pity and not with blame. In God's sight we do not fall: in our sight, we do not stand. Both of these are true; but the deeper insight belongs to God" (*Revelations of Divine Love,* chapter 82). It's rather like we do with our children, at least when they're little and cute. We can't see the trouble they cause us. We repeat like a mantra, "That's my child." They're me. I love their truth so much. I see myself in their eyes, their laughter, and even their worst actions. I cannot reject them because they're me. That seems to be how God loves what God has created.

Is the Universe Friendly?

When we are fully present, we don't accomplish presence with our head. Our whole being is present. We learned presence in infancy, but it may have been schooled out of us. Psychologists now say there is no such thing as an infant. There's only an infant/mother; in the first few years they are one, especially from the infant's point of view. Infants see themselves entirely mirrored in their parents' eyes, especially the mother's. What her eyes tell us about ourselves, we believe and become. It's a mirroring game. Prayer is much the same: we receive and return the divine gaze.

It's a heavy book, not for everyone, but *Coming to Our Senses* by Morris Berman is helpful here. He makes the point that our first experience of life is not a merely visual one of knowing ourselves through other people's responses; it is primarily felt in the *body.* He calls this feeling kinesthetic knowing, which starts breaking apart only around two or three years of age. We know ourselves in the security of those who hold us and gaze upon us. It's not heard or seen or thought. It's felt. That's the original knowing.

All the later education we might get, even a Ph.D., does not change our living out of that kinesthetic knowing. We might think we're now smart and learned, but this early way of knowing is what we finally fall back on. That's what a great gift a good mother and father are. They enable us to know ourselves at a depth that cannot be shaken.

The psychologists even say that when we first begin to doubt and move outside of that kinesthetic knowing, we take little things like Teddy Bears and dolls to ourselves. We do that to reassure ourselves that union is truth. We begin to doubt it as the subject/object split of a divided world hits us. Body/mind/world/self all start getting split up; the basic fault lines of the world become real to us.

True spirituality is always *bringing us back* to this original knowing that is unitive experience. My little sister had the classic security blanket. She dragged it everywhere — and it was so dirty! It was falling apart and shredded and she still had to carry it along. The child does not want to let go of kinesthetic knowing. Mothers give us a primal experience of life as union. My mother's eyes tell me I'm the beloved. But when I begin to see myself through eyes that compare, judge, and dismiss, then the division begins and conscious spirituality is needed.

The division has to happen. We have to leave the garden. We can't stay there, letting mother gaze at us forever. So don't look for anyone to blame or say to any group, "You took me out of the garden." The whole Bible is written outside the garden. It is only important that you have a garden to remember. Apparently in our culture today a lot of people don't. I suppose that's why Jesus says, "It would be better for you if a millstone were hung around your neck and you were thrown into the sea than for you to cause one of these little ones to stumble" (Luke 17:2). When primal knowing is wounded or missing, an immense doubt is created about whether there even is a garden. We have many such people who live with this doubt, and religious experience only comes to them with great difficulty. We can relate to God only according to the level of our human development and the level at which we relate to everyone else. Most don't know how to surrender to God. How can we surrender unless we believe there is someone trustworthy out there to surrender to?

At the end of his life, Einstein, with all of his brilliance, said, "Now I see that the only question is, 'Is the universe friendly?' . . . I have begun to discover its physical meanings but the question that haunts me is, 'Is it friendly?'" Is this whole thing out there on our side or not? Is the universe hostile or benevolent? Is it radically okay or is it not? The gift of true religion is that it parts the veil, returns us to the garden and tells us our primal experience was trustworthy. It reassures us that we live in a benevolent universe, and it is on our side. The universe, it reassures us, is radical grace. Therefore, we do not need to be afraid. *Scarcity* is not the primary experience, but *abundance.* Knowing this, we can relax and let go.

"Be not afraid" is the most common single line in the Bible. Look for yourself if you don't believe me.

As Mary Anne Williamson says in her book *Return to Love,* the "fear" worldview and the "love" worldview do not know one another. What I'm calling the fear worldview is what John calls "the world." It is "the system."

Our culture teaches us that everything out there is hostile. We have to compare, dominate, control, and insure. In brief, we have to be in charge. That need to be in charge moves us deeper and deeper into a world of anxiety. As with our attachment to the system of producing and consuming, this anxiety gets worse as we get older.

As the anxiety deepens, we begin to eliminate people from our lives if we can't control them. We eliminate the ones we can't fix, control, or see the divine image in. At the end too many of us are living in nursing homes with nobody. Nobody. We become isolated selves, living the lie we believed to begin with: it has become a self-fulfilling prophecy.

In *Coming to Our Senses*, Bernham points out that around the year 1500, there was a mass proliferation of a new invention: the mirror. After that watershed event in history, we see an increasing split within the self. People start to live almost entirely outside of themselves. America has made an art form out of it through Hollywood and Madison Avenue. We really don't live inside anymore, but we live through others' eyes. "Am I color-coordinated today?" "Am I attractive?" "Do I have a small enough waistline?" We don't live in our bodies, where we can feel our own feelings and trust our own experience. Instead, through commercials and advertisements and jingles we live in images and appearances. We let the media and passing material objects define success. The self, therefore, is always outside, and we live in constant dissatisfaction. What a tortured way to live! We suffer, quite frankly, from a lack of contact with *reality;* we lack what philosophers call ontological mooring. Contemplation provides that mooring, that contact; it is an appreciation of and response to what is real right here and now.

Until we break the material world's hold on us and reestablish contact with reality, we will never be happy. We will live our lives through these beautiful models that we can't live up to, with their perfect bodies, trim waistlines, even teeth, and zit-free faces! What a terrible tragedy that people should be seduced into imitating and desiring what we are not and can never be.

What freedom it must have been to live before the mirror and the photo. When you go into third world countries, into the jungles, people love to have their picture taken. But they pose for it so differently than we do. You've seen it. When we pose for a picture, we pull in our stomach and smile. They don't do that. They don't smile. They look serious. They usually stand erect, formal and serious. The body is as it is —right there, given to you. They haven't spent their whole life looking at photographs as we have.

We've paid a price for our technologies. The price is our soul. The soul doesn't know itself by comparison and differentiation. The soul just is. The soul knows itself through what is *now* and everything that *is*, both the dark and the light. The soul triumphs over nothing and therefore cannot be defeated because it is not in the game of succeeding or failing. It does not need to separate the dark from the light. Everything belongs.

The ego is the dualist inside of us. "It is the habit," James Carse says, "of seeing ourselves over and against someone else." That's exactly what the ego wants to do. To my ego, my wealth, my intelligence, my moral goodness, and my social class are what they are only in contrast to the person next to me. But the still center, my true self, does not need to oppose, differentiate, or compare itself. That's why it can live out of this primal kinesthetic knowing. To the extent our soul is alive, we are satisfied with the "enoughness" of the present moment and are in touch with reality.

Living out of our ego splits us off from our body. We fear the body. The teaching on sexuality is almost universally impoverished in Christian denominations. I think the reason we have done such a horrible job on the body is that we've surrendered to this dualist split. It is why so many of us, especially men, don't know our feelings. We didn't even know they were important. We moved into that basic split and we repressed our feelings for the sake of efficiency and success. Unfortunately, we sacrificed religious sensibility, too. Now it seems like something foreign, artificial, and even irrational.

When we get rid of our kinesthetic knowing, we are more efficient. We can keep pushing feelings down and move ahead with what we have to do in the next hour. There are times when that is quite appropriate, and even helpful and necessary. But not always. As soul, we don't really act. We just are. As ego, we cope with the world. We change it. We rearrange and constantly try to improve it. As contemplatives, we first stand in vigil, and then we act from that more spacious place, although sometimes we choose not to act, or not to act *now*.

The Priority of Contemplation

This may seem odd, coming from a Center of Action and Contemplation that works to improve people's lives and is committed to social change, but after eight years at the center I'm convinced that I must primarily teach contemplation. I've seen far too many activists who are not the answer. Their head answer is largely correct but the energy, the style, and the soul are not. So if they bring about the so-called revolution they are working for, I don't want to be part of it (especially if they're in charge). They *might* have the answer, but they are not *themselves* the answer. In fact, they are often part of the problem.

That's one reason that most revolutions fail. They self-destruct from within. Jesus and the great spiritual teachers primarily emphasized transformation of consciousness and soul. Unless that happens, there is no revolution. When leftists take over, they become as power-seeking and controlling and dominating as their oppressors because the demon of power has never been exorcised. We've seen this in social reforms and in many grassroots and feminist movements. You want to support them and you agree with many of their ideas, but too often they disappoint. I wonder if Jesus was not referring to this phenomenon when he spoke of throwing out the demons (leaving the place "swept and tidy") and then seven other demons returned making it worse than before (Matt. 12:45). *Overly zealous* reforms tend to corrupt the reformers, while they remain incapable of seeing themselves as unreformed. We need less reformation and more transformation.

The lie always comes in a new form that looks like enlightenment. We all say, "This is it," and we jump on the bandwagon, the new politically correct agenda. And then we discover it's run by unenlightened people who in fact do not love God but love themselves. They do not love the truth, but love control. The need to be in power, to have control, and to say someone else is wrong is not enlightenment. Such unenlightened leaders do not love true freedom for everybody but freedom for their system. That's been my great disappointment with liberals. Liberals often lack the ability to sacrifice the self or create foundations that last. They can't let go of their own need for change and control and stand still in a patient, humble way as people of faith often can. No surprise that Jesus prayed not just for fruit, but "fruit that will last" (John 15:16). A rarity, it seems.

To live in the present moment requires a change in our inner posture. Instead of expanding or shoring up this fortress of "I" —the ego —which culture and often therapy try to help us do, contemplation waits to discover what this "I" consists of. What is this "I" that I'm trying to shore up and expand? Who is this self I take so seriously?

To discover the answer, we have to wait and observe. That's what happens in the early stages of contemplation. We wait in silence. In silence all our usual patterns assault us. Our patterns of control, addiction, negativity, tension, anger, and fear assert themselves. That's why most people give up rather quickly. When Jesus is led by the Spirit into the wilderness, the first things that show up are wild beasts (Mark 1:13). Contemplation is not first of all consoling. It's only real.

But go into the closet, as Jesus says, and shut the door (Matt. 6:6). Only then, when you stop the parade of new voices and ideas, will you see the underlying and ever-recurring patterns. It is a humiliating experience. The first voices we hear are normally negative. They are paranoid and obsessive voices. They are agenda-driven and insecure voices. They are lustful and lazy voices. You will want to run, I assure you.

When we are nothing, we are in a fine position to receive everything from God.

We attempt to heal this sense of disappointment with ourselves by identifying with a positive visual image or intellectual idea of ourselves. "I am smart," or "I am good looking," or, in this country, "I am successful." "I've made this much money," "I have this degree or title." In terms of the Lord's Prayer, those are the debts and debtors that must be forgiven. We need to let go of these false self-images. They do not serve us well. They are debts that hang over us because we ourselves are both the creditor and the debtor, and enough is never enough.

Most people spend their entire lives living up to these mental self-images instead of living in the primal "I" that is already good in God's eyes. But all I can "pay back" to

God or others or myself is *who I really am.* That's a place of utter simplicity. Perhaps we don't want to go back to it precisely because it's so simple. It feels unadorned. There's no dressing, nothing to congratulate myself for. I can't prove any worth, much less superiority. There I am naked and poor. After years of false adornment, it will at first feel like nothing.

But being nothing has a glorious tradition. When we are nothing, we are in a fine position to receive everything from God. If we look at all the great religious traditions, we see they use those words. The Franciscan word would be "poverty." The Carmelite word would be *nada, nihil* — "nothingness." The Buddhists speak of emptiness. Jesus preferred to talk in images so he spoke of the desert. The desert is where we are voluntarily understimulated. No feedback. No new data. That's why he says to go into the closet. That's where we stop living out of other people's response to us. We can then say, I am not who you think I am. Nor am I whom you need me to be. I'm not even who I need myself to be. I must be "nothing" in order to be open to all of reality and new reality."

The Zen master calls this state "the face we had before we were born." Paul would call it who you are: "in Christ, hidden in God" (Col. 3:3). I just say it is who you are before having done anything right or anything wrong, who you are before having *thought* about who you are.

Our thinking doesn't make it so. Thinking creates the ego self, the self of reputation, the insecure self. Contemplation, on the other hand, recognizes the Godself, the Christself of abundance and security.

Thinking has taken over in the West. I blame it all on René Descartes. His famous phrase is "I think, therefore I am." *Cogito, ergo sum.* We called his insight, strangely, the beginning of the Enlightenment. It was exactly *not* enlightenment. Instead it was a moving into the mind and identifying with our finite, limited ability to conceptualize things in our isolated brain. What arrogance. What illusion to think that this private self could know. Today, we finally see that my history is not the real history I'm living. The real history is *our* history, and my little self taken too seriously is a false vantage point. Your life is not really about *you!* Surprising, isn't it?

I'm still carrying my grandfather's genes and my mother's unlived life and my grandmother's sorrow and my grandfather's pain. Their genes are in me. You see that on a little sparrow that knows how to carry its parent's genes and build the exact kind of nest that mama sparrow built. If a sparrow carries that much, think how much information we carry.

The private self is clearly an illusion largely created by thinking. My life is not about *me.* I am about *life!*

That's why the Bible is a social history. We're part of a much larger mystery. Don't take this private thing so seriously. The primary philosophical and spiritual problem in the West is the lie of individualism. Individualism makes church almost impossible. It makes community almost impossible. It makes compassion almost impossible. We've overdone this notion of the private self; it has become the only game in town when it's not the game at all. I need to recognize that I'm in a river that is bigger than I am. The foundation and the flow of that river is love. Life is not about me; it is about God, and God is about love. When we don't know love, when we don't experience love, when we experience only the insecurity and fragility of the small self, we become restless.

We even become violent and hateful because the unconscious knows "this is not who I am," and "this is not who we are." Thus rage, anger, and disappointment have become widespread in Western people. They show themselves in isolated individuals who pull out a gun and shoot — secularism is a lonely and desperate project. We cannot live a disconnected life with negative judgmental and violent thoughts in our hearts. We protest that we never do anything dangerous with these thoughts. But the trouble is that they do something with us. They leave us separate, isolated, and therefore false to ourselves and eventually false to others. But in contemplation, we move to a different space where we see the illusion of separateness. We experience what Sister Paula Gonzalez has called "a self surrounded by a semipermeable membrane." There's a lot of flow through that membrane — in both directions — and we need to start paying attention to that flow.

Inside and Outside

True religion is radical; it cuts to the root (*radix* is Latin for root). It moves us beyond our "private I" and into reality. Jesus seems to be saying in the Sermon on the Mount (Matthew 5–7) that our inner attitudes and states are the real sources of our problems. We need to root out the problems at that level. He says not only that you must not kill, but that you must not even harbor hateful anger. He clearly *begins* with the necessity of a "pure heart" (5:8) and knows that the outer will follow. Too often we force the outer and the inner remains like a cancer.

Jesus says that if you walk around with hatred all day, you're just as much the killer as the one who pulls out the gun. We can't live that way and not be destroyed. Some Christians have thought, for some reason, they could. The evil and genocide of World War II was the final result of much negative and paranoid *thinking* among good German Christians.

Don't harbor hateful anger or call people names in your heart like "fool" or "worthless person" (Matt. 5:22). If you're walking around all day saying in your heart, "What an idiot he is," you're living out of death, not life. If that's what you think and feel, that's what you will be, death energy instead of life force. Apparently, we cannot afford even inner disconnection from love.

In the next verse Jesus says, "Don't just not commit adultery; whoever even looks with lust has already committed it." Do you see how radical Jesus' teaching is? He moves down to the level of what is going on inside. How you are living in your heart is the truth. If your eye is your downfall, tear it out! Again, it is a matter of seeing. You must see correctly. If this eye hasn't learned how to see the truth, tear it out (5:29). The image is absolute because the need is absolute.

In the next passage he insists that we love our enemies and pray for those who persecute us. For Jesus prayer seems to be a matter of *waiting in love*. Returning to love. Trusting that love is the bottom stream of reality. That's why prayer isn't primarily words; it's primarily a place, an attitude, a stance. That's why Paul could say, "Pray always." "Pray unceasingly." If we read that as requiring words, it is surely impossible. We've got a lot of other things to do. We can pray unceasingly, however, if we find the stream and know how to wade in the waters. The stream will flow through us, and all we have to do is consciously stay there. Paul says, "Likewise the Spirit helps us in our weakness; for we do not know how to pray as we ought, but that very Spirit intercedes with sighs too deep for words. And God, who searches the heart, knows what is the mind of the Spirit, because the Spirit intercedes for the saints according to the will of God" (Rom. 8:26–27).

Enlightenment is precisely not like the layers of an onion. It's one great truth that you know in a moment, when the false self gets out of the way. You don't work up to it, it's not cumulative. It's an epiphany. All of a sudden, walking from here to there you see it. You know it is given and not created. We can't hold on to it, but we must return to it through daily prayer. Once we've known who we are in God, nothing less will satisfy us. We know it enough to believe it, even when we have to take on roles and titles and lesser definitions. For the sake of the common good, we all wear a lot of hats. We take the hat off when the role is finished. Do I know who I am apart from my role? Do I take my role too seriously? That becomes the trap. We overidentify with image, with what we think we are, what we would like to be; or with our reputation, with whom others tell us we should be. Both of them are the world of perception. We need to get back to substance and essence. God is there.

The West has been the extroverted part of the planet, the East more introverted. When I was in Japan, I was overwhelmed for many reasons. When I was in subway stations and took the bullet train down to Hiroshima with huge crowds everywhere, I noticed the Japanese don't make eye contact. That's considered disrespectful, so they look down. I thought, "Don't they wonder what I look like?" My companion said that they could tell from my feet and voice that I was a Westerner, a foreigner. They would not look at me. He explained that they live inside. It is an introverted culture. As an extrovert from an extroverted culture, it was very hard for me to understand. The playgrounds in Japan were nothing like American playgrounds. You could hear yourself. There was just a low hum of the children. I don't know how they train kids to be so quiet! It was quiet on the subway. Not a sound. No graffiti there or anywhere.

This introversion is part of our fascination with the East. Let me remind you that Jesus lived in the Middle East. Jesus' Semitic mind is more Eastern than Western. Perhaps this is one of the major reasons the Western church has often misunderstood Jesus' teaching. It happened that the Gospel went through Greece and came into Europe first and received almost an entirely Western interpretation through the teachers of the first two millennia. Now there's a longing for the missing side. We long for the whole Christ.

Abandoning Identity

The Tibetan word for identity means "holding on to your self." We keep trying to manufacture and hold on to a self as a fixed identity and defense against the unconscious. Identity makes us feel in control and superior and right, but it is largely self-created by stories we know about ourselves. It's constituted by what we like and don't like about ourselves, from unconscious scripts that we play over and over. We try to be what someone has called "a predictable somebody." We especially want to be a predictable somebody to ourselves. That's not all bad. It's nice to work with people who are predictable.

But when we have too much "I," with too much "I have a right to," then we necessarily move to a life of hatred, because all our rights cannot be maintained, as Americans think. When there's too much "I need," we are necessarily led to greed. We become a consumer culture. When there's too much "I" in comparison to others, we'll necessarily become envious. If there's too much "I am better than," it will lead to a culture of pride. If there's too much "I know," it will lead to illusion and ignorance. Isn't that ironic? Jesus says, "The person who says 'I know,' is precisely the blind one" (John 9:41).

Good therapy and good religion can enable us to let go of specific objects of hatred, envy, and greed. But contemplation, returning to the naked poor self, helps us *to let go of this "I" fixation altogether.* That's why it is so radical. What is the "I" in me that is hating? What is the "I" that is offended? What part of me is envious? Who is the "I" that needs more money to be happy? This is the "I" that must be examined and often released for the sake of seeing clearly.

This "I" fixation, the "I" that I *think* is me, is the one that will die when I die. This passing self of images and who I think I am is ephemeral and impermanent. It is revealed to be a creation of my mind, a mist or illusion. My novice master called it a cobweb. He would hold out his hand and blow a puff of air. He said, "That's Richard." Tomorrow it may be gone.

We're not going to know how ephemeral our thoughts and feelings are until we take the time to sit and observe. That's the early stage of contemplation; you notice how this feeling grabs you, how that identity grabs you, how that hurt grabs you, and you want to identify with it because in some way it gives you some ground to stand on. The temptation to do it is immense — especially if it is the only thing you've done for the last thirty years of your life. We haven't known there is any other way to live except to keep grabbing these passing images.

Again Jesus uses the image of a child to teach "beginner's mind." A child is one without ego identity to prove, project, or protect. Little children are not protecting identity yet. They know kinesthetically and respond to what is, not what should be or might be. That's why they cry and squeal with pleasure so much. It drives parents crazy, I'm sure. But that's also why there can be immediate delight. Just watch them squeal. When they see a little animal, they don't have to filter it through their heads and check to see if they like it. Nor do they ask if it is dangerous. Watch a three- or four-year-old who sees something new. He or she lets out an instantaneous kinesthetic squeal: "I like it." It's pretty, it's new, it's exciting. If only we could receive reality so immediately and so spontaneously, without our adult judgments and calculations. Whoever does not welcome the kingdom of God like a child will never enter it.

My mother told me that once when I was screaming with excitement, she said, "If you're going to make that much noise, go out on the back porch." In a few minutes I was out on the back porch screaming. I had obeyed, but I was still screaming. To this day I wonder what I was so freely excited about. Mom did the right thing. She said I could scream as long as I didn't bother the whole house. I guess I'm still "screaming"!

Salvation

Good religion helps us to heal and "forgive," as it were, these splits in ourselves, as does good therapy. But prayer is different from mere therapy. (I'm not trying to put down therapy. The trouble comes when people don't move beyond therapy.) Therapy heals our disconnections from *this* problem, from *this* person, from *this* difficult emotion. *Prayer heals our split from life itself.* It heals our disconnectedness from the deepest stream itself. Thus prayer affirms us at our core. That's why real religious conversion can, in fact, take care of years of therapy.

Salvation often feels like a kind of universal amnesty, a total forgiveness of ourselves and all other things.

To really experience the Absolute —that life is radically good, that life courses through me, and that this life is the presence of God —is to experience the essential pattern. When we are reconnected at our core, we leap over years of problem-solving and years of asking questions about ourselves. No surprise that we call it salvation, from the Latin word *salus* for healing. We shouldn't put down people who show great euphoria and excitement after a born again or religious experience. They're right. Suddenly the world makes sense for them. Suddenly it's okay, despite the absurdity, the injustice, the pain. Life is now so spacious that they can even absorb the contradictions. God is so great, so bottomless, so empty, that

God can absorb even the contraries, even the collision of opposites. Thus salvation often feels like a kind of universal amnesty, a total forgiveness of ourselves and all other things.

True contemplation, true religious experience, dissolves the fortress of "I" by abandoning its defenses. It looks out from a place of perfect simplicity. You can't stay there, I know, but if you know this simplicity once, it is enough for a whole lifetime. If the veil parts once and you know life is radically okay, then you are — to use the normal Christian language — a child of God. You are in union. There is nothing to prove. Nothing to attain. Everything is already there. It is simply a matter of recognizing and honoring and trusting. All spiritual disciplines exist to help you trust this personal experience of *yourself,* which is, not surprisingly, also an experience of God. People are usually amazed that the two experiences coincide: when we know God, we seem to know and accept our own humanity; when we meet ourselves at profound levels of recognition, we also meet God. We don't have any real access to who we are except through God, and we don't have any real access to God except through forgiving and rejoicing in our own humanity.

The trouble with much of civil religion and cultural Christianity its the lack of this religious experience. People who haven't had this experience tend to get

extremely rigid, dogmatic, and controlling about religion. It's almost as if there is an anxiety in them because
they know they haven't really experienced it yet. Missing the sense of the whole, they cling desperately to some
small part. They think that if they spin the prayer wheel
right, wear the right vestments, go to Mass daily, say the
words, and hold their hands correctly, it will happen.
That's not true just of Christians, either. In the Zen Buddhist monastery in Japan they had rituals from morning
to night. They made us look slovenly. Who knows their
motivation? Rituals are good and probably needed, but
for Christians, there needs to be a holy playfulness about
them. It's like children playing in a sandbox. You might
love the rituals, but you don't think that doing the rituals correctly, following the behavior perfectly somehow
changes the mind of God. God likes you before you do
the rituals. God doesn't need them, but *we need them* to
tenderly express our childlike devotion and desire —and
to get in touch with that desire.

The great commandment is not "thou shalt be right."
The great commandment is to "be in love." Be inside the
great compassion, the great stream, the great river. As
others have rightly said, all that is needed is *surrender*
and *gratitude.* Our job is simply to thank God for being
part of it all. All the burdens we carry are not just ours.
The sin that comes up in us is not just our sin, it is the
sin of the world. The joy that comes up in us is not just

our personal joy, it is the joy of all creation. All we can do is accept and give thanks.

Prayer lives in pure open moments of right here, right now. This is enough, this is fullness. If it is not right here right now, it doesn't exist. If we don't know God now, why would we know God later? If we don't see God now, would the eyes be prepared to see God later? The mystics say no. We will not recognize God later if we cannot recognize God now. It is a matter of seeing God now through the shadow and the disguise.

Prayer lives in a spacious place. It is free of personal needs or meanings or even interpretations. That's my fault sometimes: I want to give meaning to everything. It's my gift, but it traps me a lot. I look for meaning, but as someone said, "If you understand it, things are just as they are. If you don't understand it, things are just as they are." The mystery is to be ready to receive things just as they are and be ready to let them teach us.

Life does not care what I like or don't like. It doesn't matter a bit. If we stay in the world of preference and choice, we keep ourselves as the reference point. As if it matters what color I like. Who cares what I look good in? Or what movie is pleasing to me? It changes from moment to moment. No wonder people have identity crises. No wonder people have a fragile self-image; they have nothing solid to build on beyond changing opinions and feelings. If formerly we said, "I think, therefore I am," now it might be "I choose, therefore I am." That's not a solid foundation to build on.

The real question is "What does this have to say to me?" Those who are totally converted come to every experience and ask not whether or not they liked it, but what does it have to teach them. "What's the message in this for me? What's the gift in this for me? How is God in this event? Where is God in this suffering?"

I wish you could know Hugh Doyle, the accountant and receptionist at the center. He is a foster grandparent. He and his wife, Anne, take in little children until they can find a home. I often ask him how much sleep he has had, and he'll answer, "Oh, they woke me at two and four — another chance to learn how to love." It's important for me to hear that. We who are celibate and have time for silence, living alone, and shutting a door can give the impression that we are the ideal, that others should really be more contemplative like us. Hugh and Anne teach us that *life* itself is the necessary school for contemplation. Life is the best teacher of true prayer. Sometimes we "professionals" let the ritual become a substitute for the reality.

This moment has a message. This moment has a fullness. Even a baby crying at two o'clock in the morning. That's real contemplation. As parents know, you can't fake it then. There is nothing pious or romantic about a baby crying in the night, whereas we religious can walk outside, seek some solitude, and "feel contemplative." I have often told folks that the most important word in our title "The Center for Action and Contemplation" is not "action" nor even "contemplation," but "and."

four

Cleansing the Lens

If the doors of perception were cleansed, everything would be seen as it is. —William Blake

I think Christianity has created a great problem in the Western world by repeatedly presenting itself, not as a way of seeing all things, but as one competing ideology among many. Instead of leading us to see God in new and surprising places, it too often has led us to confine God inside *our* place. Simone Weil, the brilliant French resistor, said that "the tragedy of Christianity is that it came to see itself as replacing other religions instead of adding something to all of them." I could not agree more.

Prayer is not "one of the ten thousand things." It's *that by which we see* the ten thousand things. That's what great religion always is. In prayer we see all things in a new light. We've usually presented Christianity as an ideology competing with communism, materialism, or some other "ism." I can see why our perception of it slides in that direction, but corporate religion gets all tied up with totems and symbols and arguments about who's right and wrong, instead of holding the tension of life and death — and paying the price within ourselves for that reconciliation.

Every major religion has done the same. This pre-occupation with religion as an ideology leads to over-identification with the group, its language and symbols. Group loyalty becomes the test rather than loyalty to God or truth. Many of the hate letters I get indulge in guilt by association. "You quoted Marianne Williamson; therefore you are really a Course in Miracles person and you are not a Christian." It works the other way too. "You quoted the pope, so you must be okay." It is easier to belong to a group than to belong to God.

But the great tradition that is embodied, for example, in Thomas Aquinas, doesn't ask where it came from, but rather, if is it true. Aquinas said, "If it is true, it is of the Holy Spirit." The only question is veracity, not origin. Many people condemn the Enneagram because they say it is from the Sufis (which it isn't).* But that's not an intelligent or faith-filled criticism anyway. Group-think is a substitute for God-think. We believe that God is found only by our group. We then claim that identification with our group is the only way to serve God.

---

*Richard Rohr, *Enneagram: A Christian Perspective* (New York: Crossroad, 2001).

When "the way" becomes an end in itself, it becomes idolatry. In idolatry the religious concern is "Who is on my way?" and "Who is saying it my way?" The ones who say it my way are good; the others are bad. Jesus faced this same issue with his Jewish compatriots and told them, "Produce the appropriate fruits instead of telling yourselves, 'We have Abraham for our father'" (Luke 3:8).

The Gospel is not a competing idea. It's that by which we see all ideas in proper context. We believe as Christians that Jesus has given us the ideal eyes by which to see the real nature of reality. He does not *lead* with his judgments. When we lead with our judgments, we can't see correctly. When we lead with our fear, we can't see correctly. That doesn't mean that at a later time there isn't an appropriate point for a cautionary response or judgments, but we can't lead with them. If we lead with the calculating mind, we'll never get to love. We'll cut down and close down too quickly. The heart is unable to remain open, and we will not see God. As John of the Cross insists, God refuses to be known except by love.

The great spiritual tell us how to see clearly and keep our hearts open in hell. The moments of hell come when everything militates against the open heart. Times come when we can think of hundreds of logical reasons to close our hearts. Don't most of us do that? Some are already closed down in their late teens.

At the bottom of the deconstruction of our society is a cynical response to reality. If contemplation teaches us to see an enchanted world, cynicism is afraid there is nothing there. As a people, we have become cynical about ourselves, our world, our future. Someone rightly said, "The problem is no longer to believe in God; it's to believe in humanity." We're tremendously under-confident about what it means to be human. For many secular people today we live in a disenchanted universe without meaning, purpose, or direction. We are aware only of what it is *not*. Seldom do we enjoy what *it is*. Probably it is only healthy religion that is prepared to answer that question. Healthy religion is an enthusiasm about what is, not an ager about what isn't.

When civilization has flourished, when great music, art, and literature have emerged, it's always when human beings have felt good about being human. Human is something great to be. Being human is just a little less than God (Ps. 8:5). That's exactly what faith gives us, a kind of extraordinary dignity. It gives us a sense of our own meaning: religion calls us "sons and daughters of God." If we can do nothing else, we can give that back to the world: that we are created in the image of God, we have come forth from God, and we will return to God. We reflect part of the mystery of God. We are unique and apparently will never be created again.

When we see that the world is enchanted, we see the revelation of God in each individual as individual. Then our job is not to be Mother Teresa, our job is not to be St. Francis — it's to do what is ours to do. That, by the way, was Francis's word as he lay dying. He said, "I have done what was mine to do; now you must do what is yours to do." We must find out what part of the mystery it is ours to reflect. There is a unique truth that our lives alone can reflect. That's the only true meaning of heroism as far as I can see. In this ego-comparison game, we have had centuries of Christians comparing themselves to the Mother Teresas of each age, saying that she was the only name for holiness. Thank God we have such images of holiness, but sometimes we don't do God or the Gospel a service by spending our life comparing ourselves to others' gifts and calls. All I can give back to God is what God has given to *me* — nothing more and no less!

Our first job is to see correctly who we are, and then to act on it. That will probably take more courage than to be Mother Teresa. To be really faithful to that truth is utterly difficult and takes immense courage and humility. We have neglected the more basic and universal biblical theme of "personal calling" in favor of priestly and religious vocations. The most courageous thing we will ever do is to *bear humbly the mystery of our own reality.* That is everybody's greatest cross.

Wiping the Mirror

As we move into a contemplative stance, it becomes clear that we determine by our internal dialogue and predispositions — fears, angers, and judgments — much more than we'd like to admit. We determine what we will see and what we won't see, what we pay attention to and what we don't. That's why we have to clean the lens: we have to get our ego-agenda out of the way, *so we can see things as they are.*

We usually see everything through our own egocentric agenda. Our preoccupation is "How will this inconvenience me?" or "How will it make me feel?" That doesn't get us very far. We then twist reality so we can feel good. If our reality is negative, we will avoid that part of it. We need a broader lens, which is actually just a cleaner one. The truth is always too much for our ego. Who is ready for the whole truth? I'm not. For the thinking of the ego is largely based on fear. Fear of what I might not be. Fear of what I might see. Fear I won't be successful or accepted, or that I will be hurt. So we have to recognize how dominant fear is in our lives. But this fear is not a great big teeth-chattering fear that something is going to kill us. Our fear is in the service of all the little ways we have learned to protect our false self. But love is who we really are. We'll never see the love we really are, our foundation, if we keep living out of our false self of self-protection and overreaction. We must remember that "perfect love casts out all fear" (1 John 4:18).

The world, the system, moves forward out of fear. That's why it has to threaten us to make us play the game. We're threatened with loss of job, money, reputation, or prestige. One study showed that more than 90 percent of corporate crimes brought no financial reward to the persons committing them. They committed the crimes out of fear of losing their jobs. Another reason we play the game is the high reward we receive for staying in it. Why else would we play it? Rewards and punishments become almost the only game in town. But true prayer moves us, with great difficulty, beyond the reward/punishment mentality.

In contemplative prayer, we move into a different realm. It is not the arena of merit, of reward and punishment; it is the realm of pure grace and freedom. It is such an utterly different world from the ground up that most religion drags along the reward/punishment system since it can understand no other. The concepts of crime, punishment, performance, and reward are the only ways we know to get people in the game.

But love flourishes only in the realm of freedom. I have observed that the perennial doctrine of free will has been under major attack, particularly in the last twenty years. Free will has been whittled down to a tiny fragment. Nobody seems to believe they are free. We don't believe we have personal responsibility, that we are "able" to respond freshly and freely. Thus we play the victim or look for whom to blame, anything so we don't have to own our freedom. But Jesus, even on the cross, neither plays the victim nor creates victims. Now that's free will!

The wounds to our ego are our teachers and must be welcomed. They must be paid attention to, not litigated.

There is a dark side to the articulate psychological language that allows us to avoid all personal ownership. It's reached its low point in our current legal, family, and governmental systems. There is not a sense of personal responsibility for what I am doing and what I am becoming. Either my mother, my culture, my church, or my past made me do it. There is no healthy "I" living in the now. We are all victims by inheritance and victims of the past — which leaves little open future. The biblical concept of "sin" did have its purpose — personal ownership, responsibility, and freedom. This is good.

We have to recognize how that has changed from the generation of our grandparents. Most of our grandparents were still living in a time that had a language of responsibility. Sometime around the 1960s and increasingly since then, the language has switched. We have switched from a language of responsibility to a language of rights, which only aggrandizes the private self. "I deserve, I have a right to. . . . I have been hurt, I have been offended." These are huge debts the fragile ego tries to pay to itself. They have to be forgiven, because they can never be paid.

The private ego does not deserve all this supposed dignity it thinks it has accrued and can pull from the outside. The real primal dignity is a gift from God and is nothing that can be claimed by other people's response to me or sued for in a court of law. It is absurd to think we can get our dignity back by suing the person who offended us for $3 million. It is a ridiculous illusion. Even if we get $10 million, our soul will know that we have prostituted ourselves and we will have even less self-respect. We finally pay a big price for humiliating and aborting our own souls in this way.

In the great spiritual traditions, the wounds to our ego are our teachers and must be welcomed. They must be paid attention to, not litigated. How can a Christian look at the crucified and not get this essential point?

A contemplative posture faces reality and sees the presence of God. So there is ultimately nothing to fear. True religion is never about fear. It is always about moving beyond fear. Yet many of us were religiously trained to be comfortable with fear. Most of you reading this were given the quote, "The fear of the Lord is the beginning of wisdom" (Ps. 111:10 and Prov. 1:7). We were taught "fear of God" as a virtue when we were small children. In fact, the word "fear" in both Psalms and Proverbs means the awe that small children have for someone they honor and respect. It is not the fear of being harmed, but the awe of reverence and honor for someone we look up to and are devoted to. That's a very different concept, and the English word "fear" doesn't do it justice. To live in awe before God's wonder is a virtue. "Anxiety about many things" is what Jesus says we needn't have (Luke 12:22–32). Anxiety and faith seem to be opposites for Jesus.

A lot that's called orthodoxy, loyalty, and obedience is grounded in fear. I do a lot of spiritual direction, and when I get underneath the language of orthodoxy and obedience, I find fear: fear of being wrong, fear of being rejected, or fear of not being "in," fear of not being promoted in the church, fear of a God who has *not* been experienced. We call it loyalty, but it's often fear. Discernment of spirits helps us recognize what is really happening. Is this really loving obedience or is it fear? Frankly, much religion starts in fear, but it cannot grow or *end* there. As Julian of Norwich said, "Sometimes we take fear to be humility, but it is a wicked blindness and weakness. . . . It is contrary to truth" (chapter 73 of *Showings.*)

True religion is always about love. Love is the ultimate reality. We can probably see this only through real prayer. For love can be hidden. We don't see it unless we learn how to see, unless we clean the lens. The Zen masters call it wiping the mirror. In a wiped mirror, we can see exactly what's there without distortion. In a perfect mirror I see what's there, not what I'm afraid of, nor what I need to be there, but what is really there. In fact, some have called Buddhism the religion of mirror-wiping. It is the inner discipline of constantly observing my own patterns, what I pay attention to and what I don't pay attention to in order to get my own ego out of the way. But lest you think this is only a Buddhist preoccupation, remember St. Teresa of Avila's stark admonition, "For the most part all our trials and disturbances come from our *not* understanding ourselves" (*Interior Castle,* IV, 1, 9). I'm afraid we must learn to observe our own stream of consciousness.

What is my agenda? What is my predisposition? What are my prejudices? What are my angers? I meet people in high levels of church and society who don't appear to have asked these questions or undertaken this discipline. This discernment process is often called the third eye or the third ear. It refers to the ability to stand away from ourselves and listen and look with some kind of *calm, not judgmental, objectivity*. Science fiction writer Ray Bradbury coined the term "fair witnessing" to describe this kind of attention. This process can be brutal, but it is absolutely necessary. Otherwise the "I" that I am cannot separate from its identification with its own thoughts and feelings. Most people *become* their thoughts. They do not *have* thoughts and feelings; the thoughts and feelings have them. It is what the ancients called "being possessed" by a demon.

So we start with wiping the mirror until we can see what is objectively there. But let's go further than that: wiping the mirror until even the eye that is watching the mirror is not taken too seriously. The watcher can become self-preoccupied, which only distorts things further. So we have to observe, but also *not* let the observer become an accusing tyrant.

If we get past that temptation, we no longer ask questions about whether we're doing it right. We stop pestering our soul with questions like "Am I pure?" "Am I holy?" "Am I good?" "Is my technique proper?" They all fall away. It starts with mirror-wiping. It starts with doing the discipline faithfully.

When the veil parts and we see *love,* the self-conscious watcher, preoccupied with doing it right, just forgets the self (Mark 10:18). After worrying that I don't know about myself, a lovely question then arises. Who cares? My watching and judging don't change what is, but often become a concern with watching and judging itself. Prayer, however, is not finally self-observation but rather to "fall into the hands of the living God" (Heb. 10:31).

Have you been loved well by someone? So well that you feel confident that person will receive you and will forgive your worst fault? That's the kind of security the soul receives from God. When the soul lives in that kind of security, it is no longer occupied with technique. We can go back and do the rituals, the spiritual disciplines, but we no longer follow them idolatrously. We don't condemn people who don't do it our way. All techniques, rituals, and spiritual disciplines are just fingers pointing to the moon.

But the moon is the important thing, not the pointing fingers. We stand in adoration before the moon. We sing, Holy, Holy, Holy. We say, "Yes, yes, it is good." We are energized by what we see. And our private darkness is no great surprise. Who cares? Who cares where I am on the ladder of perfection? That's an egocentric question. "Where am I?" "How holy am I?" become silly questions. If God can receive me, who am I to not receive myself — warts and all?

I loved a holy abbot in Japan, but the first question he asked me when I sat down to get into the lotus posture (in vain) was, "How long do you sit each day?" I probably answered that I sit in my chair and read the paper! I know he didn't mean it in a judgmental way, but how interesting that technique (and quantity) would be his first question.

The Power of Free Will

As we observe our mental and emotional flow over a period of disciplined time, we recognize that we largely create our own experiences. I know this is embarrassing and some of us deny it, but it's true. We have the power to decide what each moment means and how we will respond to it. We have power when we know we have the ability to respond freely. We can decide if we're going to respond to something hatefully or lovingly. We can decide to attack or ask for the gift of forgiveness, or at least the gift of understanding.

This free decision is a real source of power and self-esteem that nobody can take from us. It's not dependent on having a beautiful body and being young. In fact, our inner power increases as we get older. When we go down to that place of pure intentionality where we are still free, no jail can imprison us. I tell that to women in jail. You can see they want to believe it and some do.

They learn that no jail can tell them they are a failure. Some become free women inside. They are the daughters of God. We must rediscover the gift of free will. I think its loss is at the bottom of the deconstruction of our society. It is at the bottom of our cynicism. When grace is no longer an experienced reality, it seems the realm of freedom is lost too.

Many liberal activist movements are trapped by their cynicism. It's so easy, too easy to demonize the other side. We see it written large in elections in this country. All either party knows how to do is attack the other side. I don't know how much contemplation our national political leaders do. They probably don't know about it. But it is dangerous to have public officials who have no inner life. They'll operate out of illusion, self-interest, power, and fear, especially fear of not being reelected. We don't have anything positive to believe in, anything that is enlightened or rich or deep. Negative identity, shallow as it is, comes more easily than dedicated choice. It is frankly much easier to be against than to be *for.*

Even in the church, many have no positive vision forward so they lead the charge backward or against. But note that Jesus' concept of "the Reign of God" is *totally* positive — not fear-based or against any individual, group, sin, or problem.

Even though the admonition *not to fear* is the most common one-liner in the Bible, our system never called fear a sin. We rewarded it, as all organizational systems will. When religion becomes an organizational system, it will reward fear because it offers control to those in management.

We have defined freedom in the West as the freedom to choose between options and preferences. That's not primal freedom. That's a secondary or even tertiary freedom. The primal freedom is the freedom to be the self, the freedom to live in the truth despite all circumstances. That's what great religion offers us. That's what real prayer offers us. That's why the saints could be imprisoned and not lose their souls. They could be put down and persecuted like Jesus and still not lose their joy, their heart, or their perspective. Secular freedom is *having* to do what you *want* to do. Religious freedom is *wanting* to do what you *have* to do.

In the silence of contemplation, we will observe the process whereby we actively choose and create what we pay attention to. That's why the first twenty minutes are usually so terrible. For the first twenty minutes only primary agenda shows itself. The agenda is how we get our juice, our motivation, what keeps us going. I sit at the Center in the morning, and my mind just starts going: what I need to worry about, what I'm going to do today, what this person is thinking because I haven't answered her letter. On and on and on. Usually about the time we're getting to the possible joy, we get up and get to work. As I stand up, I often realize I haven't let go for a moment.

When that's the case, how can we see anything clearly the rest of the day? We won't see things as *they are;* we will see everything as *we are.* It's all going to be like a jumping flea inside of us. We're not even centered inside our body. We're just living in reaction to anxieties, needs to please, and needs to avoid pain or frustration. I am not in here. I am over there.

We also live too much in reaction to others. There's something strangely sweet about negative or accusatory feelings. It's a strange way to achieve moral superiority: to feel right because someone else is wrong. We keep thinking until we've maneuvered ourselves into a position over somebody else. Now we've got righteous control over somebody else, but we have nothing beyond that control. It's another dead end. We have to train ourselves to recognize how we're giving an "affective charge" to an offense, how we are *getting energy* from mulling over someone else's mistakes. We can build a case against that person with no effort at all. We wrap and embellish and by the time our twenty minutes of "prayer" are over, we have a complete case. The verdict is in: the other person is guilty. And wrong besides. And because the other is wrong, we are right. "Scapegoating" is when we displace the issue and project it over *there* instead of owning it *here*, too. Only the contemplative mind can recognize its own complicity and participation in this great mystery of evil. The contemplative mind holds the tension and refuses to ease itself by projecting evil elsewhere.

I'm not saying we should be naïve about evil and sin; there is a place for appropriate judgments. But first we have to find the freedom to love. We must be free to say yes before we say no. Then we can make calm and appropriate judgments about good and evil. There is a major difference between scapegoating and prayerful discernment. Scapegoating is usually unconscious displacement; discernment, on the other hand, is conscious placement. Before making judgments, we have to clean the lens and get our own hurts and agenda and ego out of the way.

For conscious judgment is a necessity. We know that reality is not all sweetness and light, even though it is ultimately good. But unconscious judgment of something that appears bad (because it threatens our ego) is called repression. The process of repression presumes that there's a partial recognition of the danger of this feeling or thought or relationship. Somehow it is unacceptable or anxiety producing. I partially recognize and then deny it. But that partial recognition is the freedom we have. We can't really repress anything unless, at least for a second, our conscious or unconscious mind recognizes that it is there.

We won't be able to face reality except on our better days. It is humiliating, after all, to find the freedom to say, "We have found the enemy and it is us." But only when we get ourselves out of the way can we judge anyone else and take on the powers that be with righteous indignation. Perhaps this is the core meaning of "dying to self," as Christians and Buddhists use the term.

Fear of Dragons

Lawrence Kohlberg, who wrote some excellent material on levels of moral development, charted what each level of moral development was like, describing six distinct levels. He was clear about the difficulty of seeing reality, especially moral or spiritual reality. He concluded that we are incapable of understanding a stage more than one beyond our own. A third-level person can't make sense of what someone on the fifth level is saying. It is meaningless.

That's what we're up against when we preach the Gospel. Jesus, in Kohlberg's schema, is a sixth-level person. Many people have not done their first-, second-, and third-level work of conscience. They're really not bad-willed; they just can't understand a higher, more complex moral understanding. I've had to accept this from some who attack preaching and teaching. They're not necessarily ill-willed; they just have no idea where the Gospel is coming from. They have some growing to do yet. It really helps to understand this so we are less apt to

be judgmental of them. Jesus meant what he said: "Forgive them, *they know not* what they do" (Luke 23:34). The
vast majority of people, according to Kohlberg, remain
in the first levels of moral development. The Gospel of
Jesus will always be a minority position, as will mystical
Judaism, Islam, or Buddhism.

If we're not willing to be led through our fears and
anxieties, we will never see or grow. We must always
move from one level to a level we don't completely
understand yet. Every step up the ladder of moral development is taken in semi-darkness, by the light of faith.
The greatest barrier to the next level of conscience or
consciousness is our comfort and control at the one we
are at now.

Our first response to anyone calling us to truth, great-
ness, goodness, or morality at a higher level will be
increased anxiety. We don't say, "Isn't this wonderful."
Instead, we recoil in terror and say, "I don't know if I
want to go there." At the edges of medieval maps was
frequently penciled the warning: "Here be dragons." We
confront these dragons when we approach the edge of
our comfort level. "He must be wrong. That's not true."
That's our usual first response when we're called to a
higher level. But if we haven't been trained to recognize
our fears and to let go of them, we will feed them.

The most distressing letters I get are from people who
feel they must put you back in *their* box. They try to

dismiss or shame anyone calling them out of their comfort zone. For if you are right, they think they might have to change or admit they are wrong. But of course, they're still thinking egocentrically in terms of right/wrong and win/lose. No wonder they can't find the truth. How wonderful if we are free to say, "Could 10 percent of what she is saying perhaps be true?" That would be a win/win situation.

The greatest barrier to the next level of conscience or consciousness is our comfort and control at the one we are at now.

So let's ask for that kind of openness, to see more fully. God alone seems capable of guiding us through these transitional and dark stages. We, by ourselves, will always panic and run. So we need to recognize those initial anxiety responses and what that affective charge feels like. So we need to understand the kinesthetic, the bodily knowing. Body-responses are not always as obvious as sweat under the arms. They often involve getting in touch and starting to trust and feel. (I'll be honest: I'm not so good at this yet; I just know it to be true.) Women tend to be much better at bodily knowing than men are. We've joked about it as women's intuition, but I think it is simply the state of body and mind in union. That's been more damaged in the male, I have no doubt. We men have a harder time. Be patient with us. I suppose we separated mind from body for centuries to survive as hunters and warriors and slave laborers. To win in the patriarchal game and to succeed in the win/lose strategy, one must separate body, mind, and soul for the sake of efficiency. Men have been put in this game for centuries. To put yourself in the front lines of war you need to dissociate. That's the price men have paid for "power." We surrendered our kinesthetic knowing and, unfortunately, much of our soul.

Prayer and Suffering

The things that help us get back to integrated knowing are both obvious, and not obvious at all. Silence is helpful, especially extended silence where we observe ourselves and can feel the changes taking place. If silent, we can feel emotional changes, moment by moment. In quiet times we can tell what anger feels like in our body. Maybe that's why we avoid quiet times. Music and art can also sensitize the emotional world; they are not just entertainment. Nor are they just for "highbrows," for rich and educated people. We all need art and music and solitude. If we don't have them, emotion deteriorates into sentimentality. Advertisements use cheap, quickly contrived emotionality to manipulate us — cheap sentiment instead of honest emotion. We need to go deeper than that, which usually means suffering of some kind.

Prayer and suffering lead us to those emotional depths. They are probably the two primary paths of transformation. Both will connect us with the suffering and injustice of the world. In our prayer, compassion becomes com-passion, feeling with. In prayer, we increase our sensitivity to the stupidity of what we're doing to people. I can see why people don't go there. Who wants to feel all this pain? I certainly don't. I'd rather not know and just keep watching sitcoms on TV. Silence and suffering seem to be necessary teachers in all the great traditions. Most of us, frankly, would sooner just have some laws to obey. But the truth will feel outside the law at times. It is more grounded in reality than the law, so it will always feel dangerous. The best the law can do is point toward a dedication to Spirit. In general, *law gives helpful information, but it cannot give spiritual strength or transformation.* (Read the seventh chapter of Romans if you think this is a new liberal idea.) Without God's Spirit, we all stay inside our comfort zone and pull everything down to our own level. Religion without personal prayer experience is basically useless and maybe even dangerous for the soul. It often substitutes law and morality for those scary encounters with God, where we are by definition, *out* of control.

The longing for great religion is strong in our culture. You've seen the magazines, books, TV series, and talk shows. Everywhere there is longing for transcendence — angels, patron saints, UFOs, the paranormal, apparitions, and the Mary phenomenon. I never thought Mary would make prime time! Perhaps we are so obsessed with transcendence because after a while, secularism is boring. It's a dead-end vision; in a secular world, the universe is not enchanted. The bush doesn't burn; it's just a shrub. American culture wants to break out of secularism. Materialism doesn't name our reality adequately.

We're going to see a lot more apparitions in the next few years. Angels are going to be everywhere. Bushes will burn all over the place. It's like the soul is saying, "There is something more." *The spiritual world is hidden and perfectly revealed in the physical world.* That is the Christ Icon. That's why Jesus is so important; he makes visible the hiding place of God. His body is the revelation of the essential mystery. The material world is the hiding place of God. If we get it in Jesus, we get it. God is perfectly hidden, but once the scales have been taken from our eyes, God is also perfectly revealed and we see the divine image in all material things. If we don't, we will continue to pollute the earth, exhibit unhealthy sexuality, and probably hate ourselves.

Just as it was hard to see the divine image in Jesus, it is hard to see it in ordinary folks like us. For those of us from a sacramental tradition the essential mystery is constantly repeated in the Eucharist. For Catholic Christianity, Eucharist is the touchstone of orthodoxy. If we understand the Eucharist, we get it! It's the same mystery as Jesus. It looks like bread, it looks like wine, but we say it's more. I always say that it is easier for God to "convince bread" what it is than to convince us! Wine knows it is the blood of Christ, and we don't.

Can you see? Can you see through bread? Can you see through wine and see that it is more? That brings the spiritual life down to earth — literally. It says God is hiding in physical reality, in politics, in feelings, in childbirth and death, in everything of this earth. Isn't that wonderful? Without his hidden presence, we are in utter exile here.

When I was in the Kentucky hermitage the first time, one of the ex-abbots had been a recluse for some time, for years, really. A recluse is a hermit's hermit. The recluses come into the community only for Christmas and Easter. The rest of the time they stay in the forest alone with God and themselves. This was a powerful archetype in medieval mythology. The hermit was usually found in the woods. He was the man in touch with nature and instinct. The man in touch with God. Everything belonged for him; it was all one world. He could live with very little because it was all right here right now.

I was going down a little trail from my hermitage, and I saw him coming toward me. I recognized him since I knew him from years before. I felt it was not my place to intrude on his privacy or silence, so I bowed my head, moved to the side of the path and was going to walk past him. When I was about four feet from him, he said, "Richard!" That surprised me. He was supposed to be a recluse. How did he know I was there? He must have sneaked out and got some kind of news. He said, "Richard, you get chances to preach and I don't. When you're out there and preaching, just tell the people one thing. *God is not 'out there.'* God bless you." And he went on down the road. So I just told you what he told me to tell you. God is not *out there.*

The belief that God is "out there," is the basic dualism that is tearing us all apart. That's why we have raped the earth, why we have such poor understanding of our bodies, our economy, and our health. That's why we live such distraught and divided lives. What is worse is that Jesus came precisely to put it all together. He said, "This, the human, is good. The material, the physical can be trusted. This world is the hiding place of God and the revelation of God." We believe, for example, in the resurrection of *the body*, which says material and physical realities are a part of the mystery. It is not just an accident or a mistake or a burden. This bodily self, this physical world, participates in whatever it is that God is doing. Now even the new physics tells us that matter is merely the manifestation of spirit, *but spirit, consciousness, relationship itself is the real thing.** We used to think all the energy was in the particles of the atom; now it seems that the energy is, in fact, *in the space between* the particles!

Now it suddenly becomes easier to deal with people who are dying, because we know they are returning to Spirit. As the preface to the funeral Mass says, "Life is not ended, but merely changed." Death becomes holy, even sacramental, and so it becomes sacramental to deal with people with AIDS or those who are disfigured or handicapped. They are all revealing the mystery, and sometimes the sick and ailing body reveals it better. We need to lose this fascination with only the young and beautiful people as if youth and beauty were the only truth. We must say, "No, the truth is beyond that. That's just the start." We've got to learn to see better than that,

---

*See, e.g., Diarmuid O'Murchu, *Quantum Theology* (New York: Crossroad, 1997).

beyond shadow and disguise. Oscar Wilde put it perfectly: "Only the senses can cure the soul and only the soul can cure the senses." When you meet people from only one side, you have every reason to run.

The Cherokee chiefs said to their young braves, "Why do you spend your time in brooding? Don't you know you are being driven by great winds across the sky?" Don't you know you're part of a much bigger pattern? But you're not in control of it, any more than you would be of great winds. You and I are a small part of a much bigger mystery.

The only people who grow in truth are those who are humble and honest. This is traditional Christian doctrine and is the maxim of Alcoholics Anonymous. Without those two qualities, we don't grow. If we try to use religion to aggrandize the self, we're on the wrong path. Humility and honesty are really the same thing. A humble person is simply a person who is brutally honest about the whole truth. You and I came along a few years ago; we're going to be gone in a few years. The only honest response to life is a humble one.

Therefore, we are led to the conclusion that growth in the spiritual life (and this is surprising to capitalists) takes place not by acquisition of something new. It isn't like the acquisition of new information, which some call "spiritual capitalism." In reality our growth is hidden. It is accomplished by the release of our current defense postures, by the letting go of fear and our attachment to self-image. Thus, we grow by subtraction much more than by addition. It's not a matter of more and better information. The wisdom traditions say that information itself is not the key.

Once our defenses are out of the way and we are humble and poor, truth is allowed to show itself. It is not acquired. It shows itself when we are free from ideology, fear, and anger. "I know" won't get us anywhere. The truth is, I don't know anything. Our real hero is Forrest Gump! Perhaps he was a metaphor for beginner's mind. Only nonknowing is spacious enough to hold and not distort the knowing that is possible.

Similarly, meaning is not created; it is discovered. Our universe is an enchanted one; there is nothing new under the sun in terms of the soul. The twentieth century added nothing to the wisdom of the soul. It was all there already. It is still all there. We're not going to be appreciably better than our grandma even with all our education; in fact, I hope we're as free as she was when we die. I hope you can say "I love you" as she did when you die. The great patterns are always the same. It's either fear or love. It's either illusion or love. It's either self-protection or love. Healthy religion is always about love. All we can do is get out of the way.

five

Don't Push the River

Nothing is more practical than finding God, than falling in love in a quite absolute, final way. What you are in love with, what seizes your imagination, will affect everything.

It will decide what will get you out of bed in the morning, what you will do with your evening, how you spend your weekends, what you read, whom you know, what breaks your heart, and what amazes you with joy and gratitude. Fall in love, stay in love, and it will decide everything.

—Fr. Pedro Arrupe, S.J.
General of the Society of Jesus

I hope to help us get the mystery of faith a little clearer and more vivid in our own hearts. Finally, all we have to give away is our own journey. Our own story. Then we become living witnesses. The only authority we have in other people's lives is what we ourselves have walked and what we know to be true. Then we have earned the right to speak. We are walking a difficult path now. Our cosmic egg of meaning has fallen apart. We can't put it together yet. My generation is still *reacting* too much. Maybe the next generation will learn how to put it together. It certainly seems to be a difficult time to live, especially for younger people. Our major concern, as we talk about reconstruction, is out passion for the children. *We must believe in such a way that we give hope and meaning to the next generation.* If those of us in my generation do nothing more with the rest of our lives than so live that we give hope and meaning to the next generation, we will have accomplished a great deal. That's what our lives are for: to hand on the mystery to those who are coming after us, which means that we have to appropriate the mystery ourselves.

The final stage of the wisdom of faith is what we might call becoming the Holy Fool. Ironically the Holy Fool is one who knows he *doesn't* know but doesn't need to either. Paradoxically, that's the liberating kind of knowing we're talking about. The Holy Fool doesn't *need* to know. He obviously would like to know, but she is able to leave the full knowing to God.

I'm not saying the Fool sits in some kind of dull ignorance. I am saying he is in a state of inner freedom into which true wisdom comes. There is a kind of knowing, a kind of powerful conviction, that comes from spiritual emptiness. It comes from letting go and living out of the beginner's mind. We call this knowing "faith." It is a very *spacious* way to live because it alone can include the contradictions. Faith is the only way of knowing that is patient with also not knowing.

Small mind needs big mind for context and perspective, just as big mind needs small mind or it gets lost in mystique and abstraction.

I believe we can see a convergence of the Eastern and the Western ways of knowing in faith. The Eastern world appreciates what it calls "big mind." It's what our tradition would call unitive consciousness, or "the mind of Christ," a mind that knows and receives all things. It's a kind of panoramic awareness, a fundamental openness and clarity. We recognize that the whole world is connected, and we feel part of it.

The West has tended, instead, to emphasize "small mind." Small mind is not necessarily bad. It is just a different perspective. Big mind sees the whole, a panoramic awareness; small mind sees the individual and the parts. The Greco-Roman culture gave us those practical gifts. We can analyze, organize, and fix almost anything. This culture was the first container for the Gospel. That's the

Gospel most of us have been trained in. But small mind needs big mind for context and perspective, just as big mind needs small mind or it gets lost in mystique and abstraction. When we combine both we have mature faith. Perhaps it is more than accidental that Jesus came from the crossroads between East and West. Palestine was occupied by Romans and Greeks.

Small mind theology clarified the specifics, sometimes even overclarified. We fought over those specifics. We quarreled over who has the true Eucharist and who has the true priesthood, as if we could explain mystery. The Eastern Orthodox Church very early moved toward paradox and mystery. In fact, many of the Eastern fathers said, "if you can explain it, it's not true." They never got into analytic theology like the West did. The Protestant tradition, for all its gifts, is still a child of Western Catholicism. Like all children, Protestantism resents but resembles its parent. Protestant theology is largely in the head, which is where the West is. Protestants extended the emphasis on practical rationality even further than Western Catholics because of the period of history in which they emerged. Both East and West have their strengths and weaknesses.

The Buddhists call the small mind the "clinging mind." It wants to attach itself to everything in order to figure out everything, in order to control everything. It doesn't have a high tolerance for mystery or even for ambiguity. Small mind is preoccupied with clarity and control, as is the Roman Church to this day. It deals with specifics and prefers problem-solving. It is pragmatic and goal-oriented. This preoccupation gave birth to the great missionary church that moved out to the whole world, whereas the Oriental churches never moved much beyond their own. Though both the rational mind and the mystical mind are needed for wholeness, they are not easy partners.

I think it's soul work that will give us the compassion and patience to see there is truth in both the East and West. We need the full truth of big mind and the patient truth of small mind. We can't get trapped in either one. A lot of what is happening in the New Age movement is an attempt to get back to big mind. That's why it is so intriguing. But you've probably met New Age people you'd like to bring down to earth and nail to the floor. They often describe God in shapeless words. They have no accountability system for what they believe, so the ego can believe whatever it wants and needs. It's too eclectic. They pretend they're Indians and do channeling and shamanic journeys, but there is no accountability for the dark side of any of these practices. The church, at its best, functions like an accountability system: "If we say we believe this, then let's hold one another to it and also repent for our failures." That's not too bad. It keeps people honest and "keeps our feet to the fire," as we put it. It also includes inner self-correctives, which healthy people will use. However, I also believe religion, in its institutional form, is often the *least mature manifestation* of the living presence of Christ. Suffering and risen people everywhere tend to show forth God's glory more than managed religion.

With the exception of Twelve-Step programs, which have a highly structured accountability process, much of contemporary spirituality floats in midair. It has no social agenda or conscience, because it is not incarnational. It isn't grounded in community or history. It is too much "big mind" with no "small mind" to fill in the gaps. Instead, we need to move toward a contemplation that is socially engaged and tied to the earth. It must have the reach of big mind, but not be afraid to deal with local exigencies of building a community and addressing questions of oppression. That's an art form, because everyone is temperamentally inclined to one mind or the other. That's why I think Paul's image of the body of Christ is so healthy. He writes, "The eye cannot say to the foot, 'I do not need you.' The hand cannot say to the eye, 'I do not need you' " (1 Cor. 12:15f.). We all have to acknowledge that each of us reflects one part of the body of Christ.

Catholicism at its best found a way to do that which is often not apparent to outsiders or even to many Catholics. Inside Catholicism there has always been a huge continuum of belief and practice. In terms of managing this seeming monolith, there necessarily emerged the different orders and spiritualities. We have the Franciscan way of doing it, the Dominican way of doing it, the Benedictine way of doing it. We sometimes disagreed, but we were all still Catholic. There is room for immense diversity inside healthy Catholicism, more than most people realize. We knew there was enough temperamental, theological, cultural difference in the world so that we had to be pluralistic and pluriform to survive. We knew there wasn't only one way to look at or serve God. What we know about God is important, *but what we do with what we know about God is even more important.* Too often people think it is necessary that we all see God in the same way (which is impossible anyway), but what is really necessary is that we all follow God according to what God tells us. The fact that God has given us so many different faces and temperaments and emotions and histories shows us how God honors each unique journey and culture. God is not threatened by differences. It's we who are.

To Be Forgiven Is to Know God

If we can learn to trust God, the next movement of our soul is to trust ourselves. I've told many people over the years to trust themselves. It seems glib and facile. Yet I've received so many letters thanking me for saying that. Apparently, no one has told many Christians they could trust themselves. What an unsafe and unexciting world we have created. Jesus tells us in the Gospels, "Don't be afraid." He's saying it is radically okay. You can trust yourself because God trusts you, using your journey, your experience. Nothing will be wasted; all has been forgiven; nothing will be used against you. In fact, God will even use your sins to transform you! As Julian of Norwich heard from Jesus, "Sin shall not be a shame to humans, but a glory. . . . The mark of sin shall be turned to honor" (chapter 38, Showing 13 of *Revelations of Divine Love*).

If that's not the "good news," what else could it be? What else could be good except that kind of freedom, that kind of spaciousness, that kind of embrace from God that says your life matters? Your journey matters, and God's covenanted love toward you is always unconditional and usually unilateral. If you accept this good news, the universe suddenly seems to be a very safe place.

Why do I believe that? Because I see that's the way Jesus responded to everybody. When the Samaritan woman comes to him with five husbands (John 4:18), he doesn't start by imposing his agenda. He receives her story. Morality is always inside a narrative, always inside a context. From that accepted starting place, he calls the soul forth. He doesn't recommend that she go through

an annulment process. He doesn't check out how many
commandments she has obeyed or disobeyed. Instead he
makes her an apostle! He sends her out to advertise the
good news to the neighboring village. That's how Jesus
received people. He received the story that was in front
of him and oriented it toward light and freedom. That
doesn't mean he didn't challenge it sometimes. But if
Jesus is the revelation of the heart of God, that is very
good news about the nature of God. You do not need to
be afraid. You need not fear; your life will be honored
and used in your favor! Again, Julian of Norwich asks
Jesus the same question and he tells her, "Sin is behovely
('it had to be') but all shall be well" (Showing 13).

I believe contemplation shows us that nothing inside
us is as bad as our hatred and denial of the bad. Hating
and denying it only complicates our problems. All of life
is grist for the mill. Paul D'Arcy puts it, "God comes to
us disguised as our life." Everything belongs; God uses
everything. There are no dead-ends. There is no wasted
energy. Everything is recycled. Sin history and salvation
history are two sides of one coin. I believe with all my
heart that the Gospel is all about the mystery of forgiveness. When you "get" forgiveness, you get it. We use the
phrase "falling in love." I think forgiveness is almost the
same thing. It's a mystery we fall into: the mystery is
God. God forgives all things for being imperfect, broken,
and poor. Not only Jesus but all the great people who

pray that I have met in my life say the same thing. That's the conclusion they come to. The people who know God well —the mystics, the hermits, those who risk everything to find God — always meet a lover, not a dictator. God is never found to be an abusive father or a tyrannical mother, but always a lover who is more than we dared hope for. How different than the "account manager" that most people seem to worship.

God is a lover who receives and forgives everything. The Gospel says "you will know the mystery of salvation through the forgiveness of sin" (Luke 1:77). "Fore-given" means being given to beforehand —before you earned it, were worthy of it, or maybe even asked for it. So forgiveness breaks down the entire world of meritocracy and the notion of deservedness. Our logic of *quid pro quo* is useless in the realm of Spirit. Instead, if we are open to it, we will be led into the realm of mercy and grace —the unique world of God.

There were a number of fathers in the early church (the first four centuries) who believed in *apokatastasis,* which means "universal restoration" (Acts 3:21). They believed that the real meaning of the resurrection of Christ was that God's love was so perfect and so victorious that in fact it would finally win out in every single person's life. They were so sure about this that their thought partially gave rise to the mythology of purgatory —in or shortly after the death agony God's love will *still* get at you. You cannot resist such a love. Most forget that the original folk belief in purgatory represented an overwhelming sense of God's always-victorious love and mercy. Like many great mysteries, it deteriorated into its exact opposite.

When I read the history of the church and its dogma, I see *apokatastasis* was never condemned as heretical. We may believe it if we want to. We were never told we *had* to believe it, but neither was it condemned. More interestingly, we Catholics are always canonizing saints, pronouncing them to be in heaven for sure. They are our role models; we can imitate them. But in the entire history of the church, it has never been declared that a single person is in hell. Even Judas. The church has never said, "This person is definitely in hell." We almost hold out for universal restoration: that the true meaning of the raising of Jesus is that God will turn all our human crucifixions into resurrection. Again I quote beloved Julian of Norwich in her famous thirteenth Showing. "In fear and trembling," she asked Jesus, "O good Lord, how can all be well when great harm has come to your creatures through sin? And here I wanted, if I dared, to have some clearer explanation to put my mind at rest." And he said, "Since I have brought good out of the worst-ever evil, I want you to know by this; that I shall bring good out of all lesser evils, too."

Could God's love really be that great and that universal? Is life just a great school of love? I believe it is. Love is the lesson, and God's love is so great that God will finally teach it to all of us. We'll finally surrender, and God will finally win. That will be God's "justice," which will swallow up our lesser versions. Now the vengeful part of us, devoted to meritocracy, doesn't really want Hitler to be loved by God, do we? We'd prefer tit for tat. But does that sound like one of the parables? Read about the laborers in the vineyard who all get the same pay (Matt. 20:1–16). Remember the prodigal son? The punch line, many scholars say, lies in the parable's older brother. He symbolizes good church folk who are upset because God is generous. They are upset because God is grace and grace is apparently free. They refuse to come to the celebration (see Luke 15:28), which is always a free banquet.

We want to create a system inside of which we can succeed and win and in which forgiveness has no role. We want to earn salvation and prove ourselves superior. But forgiveness reveals both God's nature and ours. Apparently God is *actually vulnerable,* and we discover both God and ourselves in the mystery of that vulnerability. It is almost too much to imagine and doesn't lend itself to organized religion at all.

It is a mystery we are dipped into. Two-thirds of Jesus' teachings are about forgiveness. A good third of Jesus' parables are about forgiveness, directly or indirectly. Forgiveness has nothing to do with logic; it is the final breakdown of it. It is a mystical recognition that human evil is something we are all trapped by, suffering from, and participating in. It calls forth weeping, humility, and healing much more than feverish attempts to root out the evil. The transformation happens through tears much more than through threats and punishments.

If you look at your life and I look at mine, we'll both see that we have taken delight in holding people in unforgivenness. For example, people I know have talked about me behind my back, and they know I know. So I feel one up on them. Some people have betrayed us, people we know we really helped, we really loved. They walked off with what we gave them and returned with hostility. And there's something sweet about holding on to that. It keeps us up and them down. It keeps us with the power and them without the power. It gives us a strange, perverse moral superiority. But that is exactly, I believe, what God does *not* do!

Forgiveness is God's entry into powerlessness, as we see in his image on the cross. When we go into the Presence, we find someone not against us, but someone who is definitely *for* us! The saints report, "Someone else is holding me." "Someone is believing in me." That's what people who pray always say. "Someone is for me more than I am for myself." "Someone is with me more than I am with myself." Meister Eckhardt, the medieval Dominican mystic, says, "God is closer to me than I am to myself." The great ones are in agreement: the mystical Jews, Christians, Muslims, and Hindus — at that level the language is the same. God is a lover.

The transformation happens through tears much more than through threats and punishments.

Prayer is being loved at a deep, sweet level. I hope you have felt such intimacy alone with God. I promise you it is available to you. Maybe a lot of us just need to be told that it is what we should expect and seek. We're afraid to ask for it; we're afraid to seek. It feels presumptuous. We can't trust that such a love exists. But it does.

Often the imagery becomes sexual, because it is the only adequate language to describe this contemplative experience. I have often wondered why God would give his creatures such a strong and constant fascination with one another's image, form, and face. Why would God take such a risk unless it were an important risk? What is the connection between our human passion and knowing God? Are all relationships a school of communion?

These are the truly religious questions that we must dare to ask.

God's Most Dangerous Disguise

My guess is that how we relate to one thing is probably how we relate to everything. How we relate sexually is probably a good teacher and indicator of how we relate to God (and how we relate to God is probably a good teacher and indicator of how we will relate to everything else). Religion and relationships *are* one, it seems. Religion, as the very word, *re-ligio,* indicates, is the task of putting our divided realities back together: human and divine, male and female, heaven and earth, sin and salvation, mistake and glory. The mystics are those who put it together very well. Many faithful lovers, artists, and seers put it together without even knowing that they might be mystics. Sinners, on the other hand, are those who keep it all divided and dangerous without even knowing that *they* are therefore divided and dangerous.

Since we Christians have so often heard the Song of Songs, John of the Cross, and Mary Magdalene quoted in this regard, let me also offer the words of a Moslem mystic, Shams-ud-din Mohammed Hafiz (c. 1320–89), who writes Persian poetry with such integration between human love and divine love that the reader often loses the awareness of which is which. Listen to his "You Left a Thousand Women Crazy":

> Beloved,
> Last Time,
> When you walked through the city
> So beautiful and so naked,
>
> You left a thousand women crazy
> And impossible to live with.
>
> You left a thousand married men
> Confused about their gender.
>
> Children ran from their classrooms,
> And teachers were glad you came.
>
> And the sun tried to break out
> Of its royal cage in the sky
> And at last, and at last,
> Lay its Ancient Love at Your feet.*

Yes, he is talking about God's abundant presence walking through the streets of time and city, but his images come from human fascinations and feelings. Yes, he is talking about seething human desire, but he is also convinced that it is a sweet path to God. Why has this integration, this coincidence of seeming opposites,

---

*Daniel Ladinsky, *I Heard God Laughing: Renderings of Hafiz* (Walnut Creek, Calif.: Sufism Reoriented, 1996).

occurred with relative rarity in religion traditions? It is more common in native spiritualities, and a bit more common in Hinduism (witness the Hindu temples and rituals) and among the Islamic mystics. But one would think that if there were any religion that would have most welcomed this integration, it would have been Christianity. After all, we are the only world religion that believes that God became a living human body. We Christians are the only believers in a full, concrete, and physical enfleshment of God. We call it the "incarnation" and we call him "Jesus."

Jesus is the great synthesis for us, the icon of the whole mystery — all at once. "In his body lives the fullness of divinity, and in him you too find your own fulfillment" (Col. 2:9). Despite this, Christianity has relegated the body to a shadowy realm. This hardly demands verification after a cursory look at our tragic sexual state, our pollution of the physical earth, our gross, unbalanced consumerism, our pendulum swings between obesity and dieting, between "couch-potato" numbness and obsessive fitness concerns. We thought it was only the churches that were scandalized at embodiment, but now it seems to have been taken up by the media, lawyers, and politically correct therapists. "Sex" is the one "sin" in America that we are all supposed to be upset and shocked about — "while omitting the weightier matters of the Law, justice, mercy, and good faith," as Jesus said to the Pharisees (Matt. 23:23).

We are clearly not very at home in our bodies, and Jesus came to show us that it is our human and this-world experience that we must and can trust. It is our necessary and good beginning point. In fact, after the Incarnation, the material world becomes the privileged place for the divine encounter. But most of us are still shooting for the stars. We are looking at ascents and "higher states of consciousness" and moral perfection-ism, while Jesus quite simply comes "and lives among us." You would think Prometheus or Apollo were our god instead of the humble, human, "humus" person we call Jesus.

The biblical human is clearly tripartite, although this anthropology is more often *assumed,* and different words for the three parts are used; but in the end it mirrors and prepares us for the divine Trinity. It is only in a few places, like Paul's final blessing in 1 Thessalonians, that the three parts are clearly delineated: "May the God of peace make you whole and holy; and may you all be kept safe and blameless in *spirit, soul, and body* for the coming of our Lord Jesus Christ" (5:23).

Although spirit and soul tend to be confused, overlap-ping, and even the same in most people's minds, they are clearly two different parts of the human person: spirit tending toward mind, universals, absolutes, and God;

and soul tending toward psyche, experience, particulars, and "me." Without soul and body work, spirit frankly tends to be illusory, self-righteous, and ideological, which we see in the large amount of unhealthy religion to this day. "It is all in the head," as we say. Soul seems to be the *lost* element of the human trinity (corresponding to the lost sense of the Holy Spirit), and body tends to be the *rejected* element in the human trinity (corresponding to the whipped and shamed body of Jesus). As a result, we have a very anemic and poor sense of Transcendent Spirit, or God. We try to do "end runs" around body and soul to feel "spiritual," but it has not worked at all. In fact, we are finding ourselves in a major spiritual crisis in the West. The historic images that gave people access to God do not seem to be working for a large majority of our people.

Religious images were once "sexual": passionate, suffering, naked, bleeding, familial, and relational. Catholicism at its best understood this very well, especially in art and the use of language that was relational: "father," "sister," "mother superior," "brother." Sacramentalism was overwhelmingly tactile, liturgy was drama, and music was sensuous and satisfying. But eventually we hid many of these images in cathedral basements, and only the research of art historians like Leo Steinberg is bringing the older tradition to light: the still scandalous tradition of the enfleshment of God.

I know what you are thinking — and feeling: "This is dangerous stuff!" "What if it is all wrong?" "Where might this lead us?" "How do I know that this is not another excuse for narcissism, sensuality, and people hurting people?" All of which is possible, although all of these things are happening right now — on a rather grand scale, and even among Christians. As the old Romans said, "The corruption of the best is the worst." Look what we have already done with the Gospel. How many healthy, happy, holy Christians do you know? Where is the evidence that we have found the mystery "hidden with Christ in God" in the practical order? The present sexual climate is not just a result of human failure, but also of not finding an integrated and healing sexual ethic. "Don't do it" is not of itself *wisdom*, although it is probably a necessary beginning for sixteen-year-olds. But we need to go beyond such beginnings and discover a truly positive theology of sexuality.

Yes, it is dangerous stuff, but so is the Gospel itself. Just as we have often domesticated the Gospel to make it into a means of social order and control, so we have avoided the scandal of the Incarnation to avoid God "in his most dangerous disguise": this material world. If you think we are moving far from orthodoxy here, just look at that perennial touchstone of orthodoxy, the Eucharist. There it is again: Real Presence in physical bread and

intoxicating wine! "*Body* of Christ" we say, as we place
the bread in the mouths of believers. The act is intentionally shocking, sexual, oral, mystical, and momentous.
Only after thousands of "communions" does its truth
dawn on us, and the mystery of God's incarnation in
Christ then consciously continues again on this earth.
We bear the mystery of God.

The Spirit as a River

The forgiveness inherent in our faith teaches that all of
us are much larger than the good or bad stories we tell
about ourselves. Please don't get caught in just "my"
story, my hurts, my agenda. It's too small. It's not the
whole You, not the Great You. It's not the great river. It's
not where life is really going to happen. No wonder the
Spirit is described as "flowing water" and "as a spring
inside you" (John 4:10–14) or at the end of the Bible
as a "river of life" (Rev. 22:1–2). Strangely, your life is
not about "you." It is a part of a much larger stream
called God.

I believe that faith might be precisely that ability to
trust the river, to trust the flow and the lover. It is a process that we don't have to change, coerce, or improve.
We need to allow it to flow. That takes immense confi-
dence in God, especially when we're hurting. Usually, I
can feel myself get panicky. I want to make things right,

quickly. I lose my ability to be present and I go up into my head and start obsessing. I tend to be overfocused, and I hate it because then I'm not really feeling anymore. I'm into goal-orientation, trying to push or even create the river — the river that is already flowing through me.

Faith does not need to push the river precisely because it is able to trust that *there is a river*. The river is flowing; we are in it. The river is God's providential love — so do not be afraid. We have been given the Spirit. Jesus presents it as a foregone conclusion: "If you who are evil know how to give your children what is good, how much more will the heavenly Father give you the Holy Spirit" (Luke 11:13). The fears that assault us are mostly simple anxieties about social skills, about intimacy, about likeableness, or about performance. We need not give emotional food or charge to these fears or become attached to them. We don't even have to shame ourselves for having these fears. Simply ask your fears, "What are you saying to me about what is real?" "What are you trying to teach me?" Some say that FEAR is merely an acronym for "false evidence appearing real."

Ask yourself, "What am I afraid of?" "Does it matter?" "Will it be there anyway at the end?" "Is it worth holding on to?" We have to ask whether it is fear that keeps us from loving. I promise you, grace will lead us into those fears and voids, and grace alone will fill them up, *if we are willing to stay in the void*. We mustn't engineer an answer too quickly. We must not get too settled too fast. For it is so easy to manufacture an answer to take away the anxiety. To stay in God's hands, to trust, means that to a certain degree I have to stop taking hold of myself. I have to hold, instead, a degree of uncertainty, fear, and tension. It takes both practice and grace.

Ask your fears, "What are you saying to me about what is real?" "What are you trying to teach me?"

What must be sacrificed, and it will feel like a sacrifice, is the attachment and the strange satisfaction that problem-solving gives us. Don't you feel good when you've solved problems at the end of the day? We say to ourselves, "I'm an effective, productive, efficient human being. I've earned my right to existence today because I've solved ten problems." I do want us to solve problems; certainly there are plenty out there to solve. But not too quickly. We mustn't lead with our judgments and fears. We shouldn't lead with our need to fix and solve problems. This is the agenda-filled calculating mind that cannot see things through God's eyes. We must not get rid of the anxiety until we have learned what it wants to teach us.

There must be Someone to trust, there must be a prior experience of the river flowing through us or we will surely take control. Why wouldn't we? If there's not someone else in control, why wouldn't we be pre-occupied with taking control? There's really not much alternative in a secular culture. No wonder we have an entire country of control freaks. And it gets worse as we get older. It gets harder because we get used to the way we like things. We start organizing and shoving other people around to fit into our agendas.

Without this awareness of the river, without a sense that we are supported, we succumb to fear. We are afraid ourselves so we frighten others. But can we live in such a way that people don't need to be afraid of us? I wish we could do that. I wish we caused no fear in others. I wish others could feel the receiving spirit, the universal forgiving in us. One thing I hate about being a One on the Enneagram is that apparently we Ones put out a certain judgmental energy even when we don't want to. We are focused and adamant about our beliefs (even when they are so often *wrong!*).

We all want to be around people who don't do that. We all want to be with people around whom we feel safe and forgiven just by being next to them. You know you can show your darkest part to these people, and they'll still receive you. Some people have the gift in their very person to tell you, "It's okay." If they have outer authority besides, everybody wants to be around them, because their strength is encouraging. This probably explains our fascination with people of power, uniforms, doctors, and celebrities —look at our fascination with Princess Diana.

The Catholic Church was so worried that such for-giving people would not exist that it institutionalized the role in the sacrament of confession. Priests haven't always done their job well, but our official role as con-fessors is to make people *know and experience* that they are forgiven. Confessors are the official forgivers. Just tell everybody, "It's okay!" Nice job description. It's worth being a priest just to do that. I wish everybody could do it. And of course, we all can. The words always used by the church to validate the sacrament of reconcilia-tion (John 20:23) were clearly spoken to the assembled "disciples," and not just the twelve.

I remember as teenage boys we'd always line up with the young Irish priest because the old Irish monsignor was terrible; he'd yell at us. But the young priest almost made you feel good about sinning! He was so embracing and loving and would say such good things to us about God's love and how important our life was. We'd make up sins just to go in there and talk to him. As young boys we wanted that kind of male nurturing. We all do, from any place we can find it.

Personal Prayer and Social Prayer

When we learn to enjoy and trust the presence of God, we will naturally turn to that presence in prayer. When the church is no longer teaching the people how to pray, we could almost say it will have lost its reason for existence. Prayer is the ultimate empowerment of the people of God, and may be why we clerics prefer laws and guilt, though they often disempower us and make us live in insufficiency and doubt. Prayer, however, gives us a sense of abundance and connectedness.

If the church just leads us to be codependent on clergy and rituals, then we're just doing what managerial systems tend to do. (We all do it to some extent. Parents do it to their children at times.) The clergy often create a situation in which people need them so much, they can't live without them. I'm afraid some clergy — Catholic and Protestant — have done this to the people. For example, attendance at the service where the clergy happen to be in charge is considered all-important. This overemphasis on social prayer has left many of our people passive, without a personal prayer life and comfortable with "handed-down religion" instead of first-hand experience. We don't do God any favors by keeping the people passive and unaware.

After prayer, the church needs to teach people what I call "the weeping mode." Weeping is different from beating up on ourselves. Weeping is a gentle release of water that washes, baptizes, and renews. Weeping leads to owning our complicity in the problem. Weeping is the opposite of blaming and also the opposite of denying. It leads to deep healing when inspired by the Spirit. The saints talked about weeping frequently, far more than I was ready for when I first started reading the mystics. They often referred to the "gift of tears." They were always crying! Especially the Eastern fathers and mothers and those who were less head-centered. Francis cried a lot. So did Clare. In fact, they spent time crying together. St. Ephrem the Syrian said the freedom to cry was a clear sign that you had actually experienced God.

Other than the vestiges of Celtic and Oriental spirituality, with their rich emotional component, most of this tradition of tears has been lost. When the weeping mode is lost, all our grief seems to turn into anger and accusation. When the mourning that Jesus called "blessed" (Matt. 5:4) is lost, we move instead into the fixing, blaming, and controlling mode. I am afraid much of the church is there now, accusing instead of grieving. Healing and grieving services would help us a lot more than dispensations, annulments, suspensions, and excommunications.

Our awareness of the supportive presence of God is outside of and beyond our power to express in word or conceive in thought. This gift of contemplative prayer is not a way of thinking. It's much more a way of *not* thinking. It's not a way of talking; it finally moves beyond words into silence. It moves into the mystery that is too deep for words. I have said for years that our expression "peace of mind" is a contradiction in terms. I have never met anyone who is at peace who is in their mind, and I have never met anyone in their head who is at peace. Prayer must lead us beyond mind, words, and ideas to a more spacious place where God has a chance to get in.

While the prayer of words is an attempt *to express to ourselves* our dependence on the great mystery, the prayer of silence is not so much to express, but *to experience,* that dependence. We acknowledge and rejoice that we are the beloved, created out of nothing. I sit as content as a child on its mother's lap. I sit and wait until I know that truth in my body. Silence leads us to that kind of reveling in the mother's arms, reveling in the silence that follows making love. There are no words. There is nothing to say, just the knowledge that "it is good. It is very good," as in Genesis 1, the beginning of it all. That feeling of sadness is the primary gift that Jesus came to give us, even more than the great mystery of the church. Indeed, it is the foundational experience of all healthy and happy "church."

When we have the gift of seeing, of standing in the big picture and resting in God's providence, we will know how to create church in a healthy way. We'll know we need the mystery of community, of shared life, and of common social action and concern. We've tried to create church with individualists. It doesn't work. Think of your own church. It's largely individualists coming to get their own spiritual fix, and then leave. What I'm saying is really quite old fashioned: church only "works" with people who have some real life with God; otherwise it's all smoke and mirrors. It remains all inside the private ego and doesn't go anywhere. But if we have people who have experienced the great compassion, they will understand liturgy, they will understand social action, they will understand why we even need this vehicle called the mystery of the church. We are more than our private lives.

The Buddhist teaching says there are three things we must have. We must have the sitting, we must have the teaching, and we must have the community. Without these three, there is no Buddhism. They affirm these three disciplines every morning. Our tradition can affirm the same. We need the experience (the "sitting"); I think we've *under*emphasized experience. Many Catholics have thought that all they had to do was have the second two: the teaching and the community. We didn't necessarily have to experience the Holy One. The result has been an often dry, ineffectual, and disappointing Christianity.

But we need the experience, the wisdom of the ages, too. We can't start at zero. Next, we need the teaching of what is real and what is unreal. Finally, we must have the community, or we get back into the illusions of individualism. I don't want my words to encourage you to go into a private isolated spirituality where you do your contemplative sit each day but ignore the pain of the world. If we do that, we ignore the social relationships we essentially are. We are brothers and sisters to the core. We are all naked underneath our clothes, much more alike than different. If this teaching isn't leading you to that naked experience of communion with one another, it has failed. "Private" or individualistic prayer is no prayer at all. John Cassian called it *pax perniciosa,* or dangerous peace.

Social prayer helps us experience that our task is one and the same. Our goodness is one. Our suffering is one. Our sin is one, too. The great thing about being a confessor is that we get to see that we're all ashamed about the same things. We're all afraid of the same things. We are all seeking the same thing. Social prayer, or liturgy, allows us to revitalize this ultimate Oneness.

Tears, as I suggested earlier, are a kindred way of revitalizing this ultimate Oneness. So much is happening on earth that cannot be fixed or explained, but it *can* be felt and suffered. I think a Christian is one who, along with Jesus, agrees to feel, to suffer the pain of the world. But we can't stop there. Tears come just as much with happiness. When it is an unearned happiness, when we know we did not deserve this goodness, we lose words. Tears are our only response. We perhaps have two eyes because reality is stereoscopic. When we see it fully, we have reason for both immense sadness and immense happiness — and both at the same time.

When faith reaches a certain intensity and the mystery becomes utterly overwhelming, often we can respond only with tears. I think a lot of us need a good cry. But we can't manufacture it, can we? It took me a long time before I experienced it. Being of German descent, a male, and educated, I didn't know how to cry. Besides, crying is both embarrassing and inefficient. It slows you down. If I really *felt it all,* I'm afraid I would cry for two months.

We men (and all Westerners) have to work backward. We need to take the low road of Jesus back to tears. The man who cannot cry is a savage. The man's work is to learn to descend, to go down into "the tears of things."

I spent a lot of time in a nursing home over Christmas because my dad was there. I was talking to a woman who has four sons. She said, "I take my boys to nursing homes." I suggested this was a fine form of religious education. She said, "They have to learn there is something on the other end of life. We won't be young forever; we're all going to be there in a few years." The young boy has to learn that life is not all success, achievement, and ascendance.

On the other end of life, the old man who cannot laugh is a fool. (So, of course, is the old woman who can't laugh. And the young woman who has no tears is equally savage.) If we can't laugh after fifty or sixty years, we probably haven't done things right. We're taking ourselves too seriously; we have not discerned the mystery. Remember, everything finally belongs. If we can't laugh, we are probably holding our debts against ourselves and we haven't accepted forgiveness. The person of prayer, quite simply, is a person who can cry from the heart and laugh from the belly.

For me, the utter powerlessness of God is that God forgives. I hold myself in a position of power by not forgiving myself or others. God does not hold on to that position of power. God seems to be so ready to surrender divine power. God forgives the world for being broken and poor. God forgives us for not being all that we thought we had to be and even for what God wanted us to be. That is probably why we fall in love with such a God. Why wouldn't you? You would be a fool *not* to — and you will be a "holy fool" if you do.

six

Return to
the Sacred

*Murders are easy to understand. But this: that one can
contain death, the whole of death, even before life has
begun, can hold it to one's heart gently, and not refuse
to go on living, this is inexpressible.*

—Rainer Maria Rilke

When we celebrate New Year's Day, we celebrate the
rebirth of time. We wait for our God to do new things.
We wait for who we are. We wait for the coming of grace,
for the revelation of God. We wait for the truth. We wait
for the vision of the whole.

But we cannot just wait. We must pray. We say that
prayer is not primarily words. Yet prayer can be words,
and if the words come out of that empty contemplative place, then we can trust that we really mean them.
Our prayers then start naming and defining us. We hear
them in our own ears, and we begin to believe that they

state our real world, which means we can start trusting ourselves, because we are finally in touch with our true self.

We keep praying that our illusions will fall away. God erodes them from many sides, hoping they will fall. But we often remain trapped in what we call normalcy, "the way things are." Life becomes problem-solving, fixing, explaining, and taking sides with winners and losers. It can be a pretty circular and even nonsensical existence.

Instead, we have to allow ourselves to be drawn into sacred space, into liminality. All transformation takes place there. We have to move out of "business as usual" and remain on the "threshold" (*limen,* in Latin) where we are betwixt and between. There, the old world is left behind, but we're not sure of the new one yet. That's a good space. Get there often and stay as long as you can by whatever means possible. It's the realm where God can best get at us because we are out of the way. In sacred space the old world is able to fall apart, and the new world is able to be revealed. If we don't find liminal space in our lives, we start idolizing normalcy. We end up believing it's the only reality, and our lives shrivel.

Some native peoples call liminal space "crazy time." It's time where nothing looks like what we're used to, like the time after the death of someone you love. I believe that is uniquely the work of religion, to lead us into crazy time. Religion should lead us into that

space and deconstruct the old "normal" world. Much
of my criticism of religion comes about when I see it
not only affirming the system of normalcy but teaching folks how to live there comfortably. Such religion just
increases our "stuckness" in the old world, as does a lot
of poor psychotherapy. Cheap religion teaches us how
to live successfully in a sick system. And sometimes therapy teaches us how to accommodate ourselves to a world
based on power, prestige, and possessions. That's why
many people need more and more therapy or addictive
religion as they "adjust" to a sicker and sicker environ-
ment. If we do not question the underlying lies, we can
psychologize and theologize forever. As a general rule,
we need more and more of what doesn't work. If it worked,
we wouldn't need to keep increasing the fix.

"The way things are" must somehow be interrupted.
The system must be deconstructed. That is the job of the
prophet. The prophet leads us out of normalcy, dismisses
it, debunks it. I find it interesting that Jesus is called
priest, prophet, and king, in the archetypal meaning of
those roles. We have the priesthood continued every Sunday in liturgy, we have feasts and symbols celebrating
Christ the King, but I've never, in all the Christian world,
found a church named Christ the Prophet. Nor is there
any feast day called Christ the Prophet.

This may be because we don't want Christ to deconstruct the system. We only want the King who blesses the

status quo. Indeed, most religion is "legitimating religion." It is invoked for social control and public order. It tells us it's okay to live in toxic and unjust environments — just as long as you have a personal relationship with Jesus inside of the sick system. Pope Paul VI said it well: "There can never be personal conversion without also working for societal transformation."

I've never, in all the Christian world, found a church named Christ the Prophet.

Dorothy Day put it more strongly: "The trouble is, all of us still believe in the dirty rotten system." As long as we believe in the dirty rotten system, we're going to have problems. For we don't question it. We think we can genuflect before the system but go say our private prayers. But it won't work. There is probably no one more truly radical than real persons of prayer because they are beholden to no ideology or economic system, but only to God. Both church and state are honestly threatened by true mystics. They can't be bought off because their rewards are elsewhere.

For a while, this reshuffling of normalcy may leave us out of center, askew. You may find yourself a man or woman without a country. That's where I want you to be so you can find the country of God. Our old "country" doesn't make sense; we can't buy it anymore. We really can't believe it. We can't worship it as we were trained to do. Actually, this pattern of falling apart precedes every transition to a new level of faith. If one is not prepared to live in that temporary chaos, to hold the necessary anxiety that chaos entails, one never moves to deeper levels of faith or prayer or relationship with God. Notice again that almost every theophany (revelation of God) in the Bible begins with the warning not to be afraid. The fear is totally predictable; but if we give in to our fear, we will never be able to move to the next level.

Whenever we're led out of normalcy into sacred space, it's going to feel like suffering. It's letting go of what we're used to. That causes suffering. But part of us always has to die. If that readiness isn't there, we won't enter into sacred space. The prophet leads us into sacred space by showing us the insufficiency of the old order; the role of the priest is to teach us how to live in the new realm. Unfortunately, the priest too often operates separately from the prophet. He talks of a new realm but never leads us out of the old order where we are still largely trapped. (Such priesthood is ineffective, though quite popular.) In this new realm, everything belongs. This awareness is often called a second naivete. It is a return to simple consciousness. The first awareness is a dangerous naivete. As I've said, it doesn't know but thinks it does. In second naivete the darkness and light coexist, paradox is revealed, and we are finally at home in the only world that ever existed. This is true knowing. Here death is a part of life, and failure is a part of victory. Opposites collide and unite, and everything belongs.

In mature religion, the secular becomes sacred. There are no longer two worlds. We no longer have to leave the secular world to find sacred space because they've come together. That was the significance of the temple veil rending when Jesus died. The temple divided reality into the holy world inside and the unholy world outside. That's why Jesus said the temple had to fall. "Not a stone shall stand on a stone." Our word "profane" comes from the words *pro* and *fanum,* which mean "outside the temple." Teilhard de Chardin said there is nothing profane for those who have learned how to see. There is only one world, and it's the supernatural one. There is no "natural" world where God is not. It is all supernatural. All the bushes burn now if you have seen one burn. Only one tree has to fill up with light and angels, and then you never see trees the same way again. That's the true seeing that we call contemplation.

Unfortunately, even if we have once seen, we lose our full vision repeatedly. It is hard to remain awake even after having been once awakened. That's why we keep going back to the well to wash our eyes. We need to refresh our seeing. We forget. We start clinging and protecting. Unless there is a readiness to let go, we will not see the vision of the whole again. God cannot be seen through such a small and dirty lens.

I can see why we use the language of "born again." The great traditions seem to say the first birth is not enough. We not only have to be born, but remade. The remaking of the soul and the refreshing of the eye is the return to simplicity. It has to be done again and again, and somehow it feels like starting over each time. No wonder we speak of "beginner's mind."

There is no nonstop flight from simple consciousness to enlightenment. We must go through the transformational liminal stages often. That process feels complex and like we are falling apart. In one sense it is; as we move outside our comfort zone, we feel lost and confused for a while. Somehow we have to allow the dissolution of our previous ways of experiencing reality. This often entails a certain inner disillusionment, which it is usually forced on us by sin, failure, betrayal, and loss. Who of us would have the courage to go there alone? St. Augustine connects the inner journey with the journey toward God. He could be called the father of subjectivity in the Western church: "I was admonished to return to my own self, and with you to guide me, I entered into the innermost part of myself, and I was able to do this because you were my helper" (*The Confessions,* VII, 10). With God as helper we can *transform* our sadness into strength and even joy. Otherwise, we will normally *transmit* it to those around us.

Embracing the Shadow

Transformation is radically unsettling. We prefer a static, predictable state. To achieve our resting place in "normalcy," we tend to overidentify with one part of ourselves. We reject our weaknesses and we overwork our strengths. We all do. It makes sense. Why do what we are poor at, especially in the first half of life when winning is so important? So we ignore our true character to accommodate to what society names as successful. Then we're trapped. Ernest Becker calls it "the character lie" whereby we try to defy and deny death. I'm sure that's the basis of much neurosis; many people are living out of the culture's agenda, becoming who they are "supposed" to be instead of who God made them.

I'm respectful of therapy and make use of it, but I want to use it now as a point of comparison to transformation. Much therapy today is a needed way of dealing with our problems. On the level that we can solve our problems, most problems are psychological in nature. But, in fact, most solutions are spiritual. Therefore we have to eventually move from trying to solve them (which is good and needed) to knowing that we cannot finally solve them at the level that matters. Maybe we can only forgive them, embrace them, or weep over them.

This movement from the psychological to the spiritual feels like a loss of power. It *is,* for the ego-self. But it is *not* for the true self. To succeed in the first half of life we usually have to deny our shadow and unacceptable self. The burden of the second half of life is often the reclaiming of what we have denied, feared, and rejected.

Therefore, the shadow for many of us middle-class, successful, first-world white people is not what the church usually points to. The church (and now lawyers and the media) usually point to sex. But that's usually not the issue. Our shadow is *failure itself.* Look at what we scorn. It's powerlessness and poverty. That's what we scorn. We are desperately afraid of having no power and not looking good. We fear poverty, and we fear being ordinary. It looks like failure in a success-driven culture.

Nonviolence, nonpleasure, and nonaggression are also part of our American shadow. These are the things that we avoid to create our character armor. We lust after the kind of aggression that allows us to be dominant and powerful. We settle for a certain kind of pleasure that really isn't joyous. Sometimes pleasure, as a liminoid experience, is the avoidance of joy. It is to entertain one part of our body, perhaps, but at the price of the inner glow and juice of our whole being. And poverty is the ultimate shadow for many of us. We cannot imagine being happy without our money. We would be petrified to be without our many options. We've substituted freedom of choice for the freedom of the soul, which alone gives spiritual joy.

We need to look for our shadow, what we dismiss and what we disdain. Look at what we've spent our whole life avoiding. We don't want to look unsuccessful. That's our shadow. If we fear looking weak, that is our shadow. I can see why my father, Francis, intentionally countered the way the West was moving. He moved entirely into the shadow self and said, "Here is where I will rejoice. I will delight in nonpower, nonaggression, nondomination, nonpleasure, nonwealth, nonsuccess." He lived so close to the bottom of things that he could never fall very far. Now that is freedom!

As we integrate and forgive our shadow, life looks different. We see what we have never dared look at before. Biblical faith feels like giving up our eyes and seeing things as God sees them. God doesn't look at our faults, but at the places in us that are trying to say "yes." You do the same with your own children. You see beyond the "no" to the abiding "yes." God sees the divine image in you as you see your image in your children. God looks at us and sees that we reflect the divine image. We move, we smile, we play in God just like children reflect their parents in every move and smile (and even flaw). Julian of Norwich says it so well: "God judges us by our true inner nature, which is always kept whole in him, safe and sound forever. And this judgment comes from his rightfulness, whereas we judge by the outward, change-able nature. . . . In his judgment I saw him assign no whit of blame to us" (chapter 45, Showing 14, *Revelations of Divine Love*). How different Christianity would be if it had only believed in such healing love!

All the world can give us is small mind. But small mind, without the unitive experience of big mind, makes us feel unbearably alone. We feel lost, existentially guilty, and often fragile and powerless. A lot of guilt is not about this or that particular sin; it's really a guilt *about not hav-ing lived yet.* We call that essential or primal guilt. It's deeper than guilt for an offense we can name. It feels like shame, not about anything in particular, but about who we are and who we aren't. Many of us suffer from this primal guilt and this essential shame.

There is a certain fear of death that comes from not having lived yet. I had to face death myself when I had cancer a few years ago. I don't think I was afraid of death at that time, but I also knew *I had already lived.* Once you know you have touched upon this mystery of life, you are not afraid of death. But there's an existential terror about losing what you've never found. Something in me says, "I haven't done 'it' yet." I haven't experienced the stream of life yet. I haven't touched the real, the good, the true, and the beautiful — which is, of course, what we were created for.

It's heaven all the way to heaven. And it's hell all the way to hell. Not later, but now.

When we know we have experienced the stream of life, we will be able to lie on our deathbed like Francis and say, "Welcome, sister death." I'm not afraid to let go of life, because *I have life.* I am life. I know life is somehow eternal, and another form is waiting for me. It is the last threshold, but I've been over this threshold before. I think this is what Paul means when he speaks of "reproducing the pattern of his death and knowing the power of his resurrection" (Phil. 3:10). It is an actual pattern that we must live through at least once — and then we understand something forever.

But if we've never lived, we will be terrified of death. We will have no assurance that this isn't the end. Jesus said, "I am life." He came to promise us that this mystery called life and love is eternal, but that we have to enter into it *now*. It's heaven all the way to heaven. And it's hell all the way to hell. Not later, but now.

If we don't touch upon life now, how do we think we'll believe in it afterward? Yahweh, the God of Israel, is defined as "the one who creates life out of death and calls into being what does not exist" (Rom. 4:17). Give me your failure, he says I will make life out of it. Give me your broken, disfigured, rejected, betrayed body, like the body you see hanging on the cross, and I will make life out of it. It is the divine pattern of transformation, and it never seems to change. We'll still be confused, but not so confused with our confusion. We'll still have our little anxieties and fears, but we will not be so afraid of our fears. We'll still experience weakness but will not be so weakened by our weakness.

We'll still be handicapped and terribly aware of our wound, but as St. Augustine says, "In my deepest wound I see your glory and it dazzles me." Our wound is our way through. Or as Julian also put it, at the risk of shocking us, "God sees the wounds, and sees them not as scars but as honors. . . . For he holds sin as a sorrow and pain to his lovers. He does not blame us for them" (chapter 39, Showing 13, *Revelations of Divine Love*). We might eventually thank God for our wounds, but usually not until the second half of life.

Alcoholics talk like this. They tell me, "It was the worst possible thing. I ruined my marriage and lost my job and hurt my kids. It doesn't make a bit of sense, but it is the greatest thing that ever happened to me — that I was a drunk." That's what we mean by everything belongs! When an old drunk can say alcoholism was the greatest gift God ever gave him, then everything surely belongs. Logically that doesn't make any sense, but theo-logically it does. What a shame that he lost his marriage and hurt his kids. He wishes he could undo it. But because of that experience, his heart was finally broken open. Now he can go back to his wife and children with compassion and freedom. Isn't that better than so-called "doing it right" and becoming more rigid, self-righteous, and ignorant with each passing year? I admit it is a great mystery and a profound paradox: "He sees them not as wounds but as trophies," Julian says. Quite awesome —and understandable only in the eternal economy of grace.

A lot of people have done it "all right." But when you look at them you say to yourself, "If that's salvation, I don't know that I want to be saved." If those are the people in heaven, I don't want to go there! Is that what heaven is going to be like? A bunch of superior people who tell you when you're wrong all the time? Is that the life Jesus promised? That can't be it.

On the other side, you meet these little souls who have been eaten up and spit out by life. Yet their eyes shine. I saw so many shining eyes in the Philippines. The Filipinos are a people with so little. I celebrated a Sunday Mass in a squatter's camp. Shacks all around. Yet they were so excited that "Fodder" was coming. The kids met me to lead me into the barrio. Out of these shacks came kids in perfectly clean clothes. I don't know how the mothers kept them so clean. They were all dressed up for Sunday Mass. The boys all got their guitars, and it was the big event of the week. They have something we have lost.

I felt like telling them, "You live in a 'dump' by our standards, but do you know what you have? You have a culture that's not deconstructed. You're not cynical like we are. You're all smiling. Why should you be smiling? You don't have any reason to smile. You live in a shack! It smells like garbage. But you have father and mother and clear, simple identity." That's all children need for security and happiness. All the time I was celebrating Mass they were lighting candles around me and setting out statues, all this old-fashioned devotional Catholicism. We'd throw it all out as pious religiosity. But they're smiling and a lot of us aren't.

I don't know who trained them to do this, but you constantly feel your hand taken by the little Filipino children. They take your hand and put it to their head. They don't *ask* you to bless them. *They take it from you.* It made me weep. For they have their souls yet! They have light, they have hope. The little children call you "Fodder, Fodder," and I think when they pull blessings out of you, blessings really come forth. They are ready for the blessing. They believe in the blessing, and you are not really sure if it was there until they saw it, expected it, and demanded it. These are the blessed of the earth who usually don't need to be taught contemplation. Suffering seems to teach them.

Walking the Third Way

In talking about letting go of the ego's needs and accomplishments and the need to be less in control, I could be interpreted as overemphasizing detachment. But when you look at Jesus on the cross, you see that Christianity is a religion of *attachment.* Jesus says to love and pay the price for it. The soul always attaches. It falls in love. Look at the image of the Sacred Heart of Jesus. His heart is out in front. Maybe it's terrible art, but it's great theology. The heart is given, and the price is paid. When we attach, when we fall in love, we risk pain and we will always suffer for it. The cross is not the price that Jesus *had* to pay to talk God into loving us. It is simply where love will lead us. Jesus names the agenda. If we love, if we give ourselves to feel the pain of the world, it will crucify us. (This understanding of the crucifixion is much better than thinking of Jesus as paying some debt to an alienated God, who needs to be talked into loving us.)

We'd like to remain in an aloof, Zen-like detachment, but that's not the Christian way. The Christian way is to attach. As we start paying the price, we start realizing that we are not loving very well. We are only meeting our own needs. Our new word for this is "codependency." This kind of love is impure and self-seeking. A lot of what we call love today is not love at all.

We have to pull back and learn the great art of detachment, which is not aloof, but the purifying of attachment. Our religion is not pure detachment or pure attachment; it's a dance between the two. Another set of images for this reality is the desert and the city. Jesus moves back and forth between desert and city. In the city, he feels himself losing perspective, love, and center and has to go out to the desert to see the real again. And when he is alone in the desert, his passionate union with the Father drives him back to the pain of the city.

We go back to be purged by God's mercy and regrafted to the vine; we go back to the well until we know what the real is, and then we return to the city. The work of the soul is attachment; the work of spirit is often detachment. Without the art of detachment, the culture becomes addictive, and we have massive codependency. We have people enmeshed in one another who do not know their own identities. They have nothing to give because there is no "I" there. Without attachment, however, there is no risk, no passion, no compassion, no social justice, no holding the tension and collision of opposites.

This tension or dance between attachment and detachment is often called the Third Way, a concept I discussed earlier. It is the middle way between flight and fight, as Walter Wink describes it. Some prefer to take on the world, to fight it, to change it, fix it, and rearrange it. Others, the "flight" people, deny there is a problem. "Everything is beautiful," they say, and look the other way. Both of them avoid holding the tension, the pain, and the essentially tragic nature of human existence.

The contemplative stance is the Third Way. We stand in the middle, neither taking the world on from the power position nor denying it for fear of the pain it will bring. We hold the realization, seeing the dark side of reality and the pain of the world, but *we hold it until it transforms us,* knowing that we are complicit in the evil and also complicit in the holiness. Once we can stand in that third spacious way, neither fighting nor fleeing, we are in the place of grace out of which newness comes. Creativity comes from here, and we can finally do a new thing for the world. When our ego stops getting hooked, when it's not our agenda, then we can hope ours is the agenda of God. We can stop building our kingdom and become *usable* in the kingdom of God.

The Third Way is the way of wisdom. It's a lonely, perhaps narrow path, because almost everybody takes the
other two ways: flight or fight. The usual path for liberals
is to fight. "Let's fix and change it." But they too often
become a mirror image of what they oppose. Conservatives tend to take flight by denying there is a problem.
They love to quote the saying "the poor you will always
have with you," and then assert that "our job is just to
get it right with Jesus." They're frequently into massive
denial of institutional evil, except for the security systems they build. The wealthy never see how 90 percent
of the world lives. That's dangerous illusion. It's been one
of the great sins of the Catholic countries. They look at
the cross but don't realize what the cross is saying. That is
true for both liberals and conservatives: the liberals deny
the vertical arm of the cross (transcendence and tradition); the conservatives deny the horizontal (breadth
and inclusivity).

Our Center for Action and Contemplation has been
called a school for prophets. That's what we want it to
be. The prophets in Israel are always Israelites, good and
proud Jews who believe in their tradition. They are not
deconstructed persons outside Judaism throwing rocks
back at the temple. They love the temple and the law.
But they see it all the way through, they see, as Jesus
did, the real *purpose* of the law and temple. The prophet
combines the best of the conservatives and the best of

the progressives. Yet that usually makes them "radicals" and unacceptable in either camp.

Jesus was completely immersed in his Judaic tradition. He didn't start with some idea he made up. Nor can we. We cannot carry the prophetic charism unless we are rooted and grounded and accountable somewhere. That's why most liberals are "limosine liberals" and not true Gospel "radicals." They pick and choose a little bit from this system and a bit from that one. There's frequently no place where they are accountable and sur-rendered and grounded. As Gandhi said, you have to dig one deep well, not many shallow ones. So in one sense I don't believe in prophets who are not conservative in that sense. Prophets must be grounded in the Great Tra-dition of wisdom. Our grandparents were not stupid. The truth is already there. The patterns of the soul are not new, and our century hasn't discovered anything new in terms of how death is transformed into life. The price is still the same: "to create one new person from us who had been two ... reconciling both of us to God in one body through the cross which puts all enmity to death" (Eph. 2:15–16). *It's the only truly transformative pattern in human history.*

That's a weakness for Americans because we are a people without a history. We don't appreciate tradition. As Henry Ford said, "All history is bunk." He was a quin-tessential American. We think we don't need the past;

all we need is pragmatic problem-solving. But this is all small mind, no big mind. That's the vision we've taken on as a country, or perhaps I should say, *lack* of vision. We seldom look at the long-haul patterns of life and death. We are short-run people.

The prophets were true traditionalists and not just self-serving "conservatives." (The Great Tradition has been called "the living faith of the dead," while much traditional*ism* is "the dead faith of the living.") All the prophets of Israel had an overwhelming experience of absoluteness. One alone is absolute. That's the core of Jewish monotheism. Only One is good, One is real. That experience of the overwhelming One thing relativizes everything else, including the structures of religion: papacy, Bible, sacraments, and our interpretation of each of those. They are all true, but they are symbolic, pointing to something beyond themselves. All religion is metaphor and symbol, which is not to dismiss religion at all. There is no other way we can know the mystery. Symbol and metaphor are the only way we can see the spiritual and the transcendent.

To be prophets we must first see in ourselves what we see in others: good and bad. I hate consumerism because I recognize I'm an American consumer. (I love my nice Christmas sweater.) But if we hate it "over there" and not in ourselves, we become self-righteous. The inner movement is to recognize the sinner in ourselves and to forgive ourselves for our sin. This *does* mean that we recognize our sin as sin, we see its evil and its damage, and we want to change. Our religious word for this is "repentance." Then we don't stand apart from anybody else, or above or in judgment of anybody else. We all share the same divine image, which is also to honor the good in both myself and in the would-be opponent.

Finally, we have to wait and ask for the grace to respect and honor people who don't agree with us. When people shoot people in abortion clinics, we know they're not true prophets. That is far from the prophetic charism. They may have started out with one great insight: the meaning of human life. They're clearly right on that. They've seen the divine image in the fetus of a human and in all that is created. That's a great beginning. But then they get snagged by self-image. Without further spiritual work they overidentify with their superiority, their righteousness, and the evil of the other, and then they become blind. They end up shooting another divine image. They're not credible prophets. If we hate people who don't agree with us, if we feel righteous and superior to those who have different politics, we're not in the Spirit. Until that grace is given, we should not presume we have a prophetic charism. When we have the prophetic charism, we don't inflict pain on "them"; we hold the pain in ourselves. We absorb the pain; we don't project it or avenge the evil we see. We surrender to the realization that we are also complicit in the evil of the world. It's just a matter of when and where and how.

Before enlightenment, all fear, judgment, and criticism is stated in the second person: "you are." After enlightenment, we join Jesus on the cross and all criticism is henceforth stated in the first person: "we are."

coda and conclusion

A Contemplative Seeing of the Doctrine of the Cross

I believe that the entire biblical tradition and the personal prayer journey both lead us to the same conclusion about what is happening in human history and how we can be used as instruments for the healing and transformation of that history. It is the essential and paradoxical mystery of the cross, which I do not believe the rational and calculating mind will ever come to by itself. Let me try to say in succinct and new ways — so you can hear the fresh and revolutionary character of my assertions — what, I believe.

- God is to be found in *all things*, even and most especially in the painful, tragic, and sinful things, exactly where we do not want to look for God. The crucifixion of the God-Man is at the same moment the worst thing in human history and the best thing in human history.

- Human existence is neither perfectly consistent (as rational and control-needy people usually demand it be), nor is it incoherent chaos (what cynics, agnostics, and unaware people expect it to be); instead, *human life has a cruciform pattern.* It is a "coincidence of opposites" (St. Bonaventure), a collision of cross-purposes; we are all filled with contradictions needing to be reconciled.

- The price that we pay for holding together these opposites is always some form of crucifixion. Jesus himself was crucified between a good thief and a bad thief, hanging between heaven and earth, holding on to both his humanity and his divinity, a male body with a feminine soul, expelled as the problem by both religion and state. Yet he rejected none of these, but "reconciled all things in himself" (Eph. 2:10).

- Christians call this pattern "the paschal mystery": true life comes *only* through journeys of death and rebirth wherein we *learn who God is for us.* Letting go is the nature of all true spirituality and transformation, summed up in the mythic phrase: "Christ is dying. Christ is risen. Christ will ever come again."

- We should not be surprised or scandalized by the sinful and the tragic. Do what you can to *be* peace and to *do* justice, but never expect or demand perfection on this earth. It usually leads to a false moral outrage, a negative identity, intolerance, paranoia, and self-serving crusades against "the contaminating element," instead of "becoming a new creation" ourselves (Gal. 6:15).

- We must resist all utopian ideologies and heroic idealisms that are not tempered by patience and taught by all that is broken, flawed, sinful, and poor. Jesus is an utter *realist* and does not exclude the problem from the solution. Work for win/win situations. Mistrust all win/lose dichotomies.

- The following of Jesus is not a "salvation scheme" or a means of creating social order (which appears to be what most folks want religion for), as much as it is *a vocation to share the fate of God for the life of the world.* Jesus did not come to create a spiritual elite or an exclusionary system for people who "like" religion, but he invited people to "follow" him in bearing the mystery of human death and resurrection (an almost nonreligious task, but one that can be done only "through, with, and in" God).

- Those who agree *to carry and love what God loves,* which is both the good and the bad of human history, and to pay the price for its reconciliation within themselves — these are the followers of Jesus — the leaven, the salt, the remnant, the mustard seed that God can use to transform the world. The cross is the dramatic image of what it takes to be such a *usable* one for God.

· These few are enough to keep the world from its path toward greed, violence, and self-destruction. *God is calling everyone and everything to Himself* (Gen. 8:16–17, Eph. 1:9–10, Col. 1:15–20, Acts 3:21, 1 Tim. 2:4, John 3:17). God just needs some *instruments and images* who are willing to be "conformed unto the pattern of his death" and transformed into the power of his resurrection (Phil. 3:10). They are not "saved" as much as chosen, used, purified, and beloved by God — just like Jesus, who did it first and invited us to "the great parade."

· Institutional religion is *a humanly necessary but also immature manifestation* of this "hidden mystery" by which God is saving the world. History seems to make both the *necessity* and the *immaturity* of religion glaringly apparent, which upsets both progressives and conservatives. Institutional religion is never an end in itself, but merely a wondrous and "uncertain trumpet" of the message.

- By God's choice and grace, many seem to be living this mystery of the suffering and joy of God who do not formally belong to any church. (Gandhi, Simone Weil, Etty Hillesum, and Nelson Mandela are just a few examples.) And many who have been formally baptized have never chosen to "drink from the cup that I must drink or be baptized with the baptism that I must be baptized with" (Mark 10:38). They have the right words but not the transformative experience.

- The doctrine, folly, and image of the cross is the great clarifier and truth-speaker for all of human history. We can rightly speak of being "saved" by it. *Jesus Crucified and resurrected is the whole pattern revealed, named, effected, and promised for our own lives.* If we can say yes to this vulnerable face of God, there will be no more surprises for our mind and no more victims for history. I personally do not believe that Jesus came to found a separate religion as much as he came to present a universal message of vulnerability and foundational unity that is necessary for all religions, the human soul, and history itself to survive. Thus Christians can rightly call him "the Savior of the World" (John 4:42), but no longer in the competitive and imperialistic way that they have usually presented him. By very definition, vulnerability and unity do not compete or dominate. In fact, they make both competition and domination impossible. The cosmic Christ is no threat to anything but separateness, illusion, domination, and any imperial ego. In that sense, Jesus, the Christ, is the ultimate threat, but first of all to Christians themselves. Only then will they have any universal and salvific message for the rest of the earth.

- The contemplative mind is the only mind big enough to see this, and the only kind of seeing that is surrendered enough to trust it. The calculative mind will merely continue to create dualisms, win/lose scenarios, imperial egos, and necessary victims. It cannot get out of its own illogical loop. Einstein put it this way: "No problem can be solved by the same consciousness that caused it."

- God has given us a new consciousness in what we call "prayer" and an utterly unexpected, maybe even unwanted, explanation or reality in what we call "the cross."

Guide for Reflection

*This guide, prepared by Crossroad, may be used
for group discussion and private reflection.*

Center and Circumference

"If the circumferences of our lives were evil, it would be easier to moralize about them" (p. 13). Name some examples of the "circumferences" of your life. In what ways do they seem to take your attention away from what's essential?

"You have to develop an ego before you can let go of it" (p. 23). In what ways do people seek their identities in groups and belonging? What do you think it means to live through God, living from our center so that "everything belongs"?

Vision of Enchantment

"We have to learn to see what is there" (p. 30). How might prayer, a "way of living in the Presence," help you see in this new way?

"When we have too many words, we tend not to value them, even if they might contain life for us" (p. 39). Where in your own life do you encounter the most words? Do words ever overwhelm you? What words do you continue to value?

"We aren't born again. We are born again and again and again" (p. 52). Reflect on the way you view religious experience. Does it leave space to experience God as "patient"?

Ego and Soul

"Try to realize that everything is right here, right now" (p. 60). Take a moment to reflect on these words. What beliefs about your past and future would change if you came to accept this idea?

"After eight years at the [Center of Action and Contemplation] I'm convinced that I must primarily teach contemplation" (p. 73). Think about some of the social reforms mentioned by Rohr in this chapter. In what way can they sometimes be "head" answers that don't transform consciousness?

"All that is needed is surrender and gratitude" (p. 89). Describe in your own words the meaning of playful prayer.

Cleansing the Lens

"When civilization has flourished, when great music, art, and literature have emerged, it's always when human beings have felt good about being human" (p. 96). Think about the people in your daily life — coworkers, family, friends. Who tends to believe in the dignity of being human? How do people express that dignity in their own lives?

"It is frankly much easier to be against than to be *for*" (p. 107). Think of examples of the divisive practices in politics and religion. How do these compare with the freedom of contemplation?

"You and I came along a few years ago; we're going to be gone in a few years. The only honest response to life is a humble one" (p. 120). How could this awareness of our short time on earth affect the way we live? The way we pray?

Don't Push the River

"What we know about God is important, but *what we do with what we know about God is even more important*" (p. 128). What does the diversity of healthy religions say about God, who is "not threatened by differences"?

"How we relate to one thing is probably how we relate to everything" (p. 136). Reflect on how you relate to

God, to things, and, sexually, to other people. Can you see a pattern in your own relations and those of people around you?

"Without this awareness of the river, without a sense that we are supported, we succumb to fear" (p. 145). How in your own life have you begun to trust the presence of God? What role can prayer play in your life?

Return to the Sacred

"Part of us always has to die" (p. 158). What part of yourself do you find dying when you enter a sacred space?

"If we've never lived, we will be terrified of death" (p. 165). How do you view death? Do you know that life is eternal?

"Our religion is not pure detachment or pure attachment; it's a dance between the two" (p. 170). Reflect on these words in light of the title of the book, "Everything Belongs."

About the author

Richard Rohr, O.F.M., is a Franciscan priest of the New Mexico Province. He was the founder of the New Jerusalem Community in Cincinnati, Ohio, in 1971, and, in 1986, the Center for Action and Contemplation in Albuquerque, New Mexico, where he presently serves as Founding Director. The Center is intended to serve a dual purpose, not only as a radical voice for peaceful, non-violent social change but also as a forum for renewal and encouragement for the individual who seeks direction from and understanding of God's will and love.

Richard was born in 1943 in Kansas. He entered the Franciscans in 1961 and was ordained to the priesthood in 1970. He received his Master's Degree in Theology from Dayton that same year. He now lives in a hermitage behind his Franciscan community in Albuquerque and divides his time between local work and preaching and teaching on all continents. He is well known for his numerous audio and video tapes and for his articles in the Center's newsletter, *Radical Grace*. He is a regular contributing editor/writer for *Sojourners* magazine and recently published a seven-part Lenten series for the *National Catholic Reporter*. He has a best-selling tape series called *The NEW Great Themes of Scripture*. Fr. Rohr has authored several books in the areas of male spirituality, the use of the Enneagram in spiritual direction, and scriptural commentary. He is working on a book on male initiation.

OTHER TITLES BY
RICHARD ROHR

SIMPLICITY
The Art of Living

"Rohr's kind of contemplation is an adventure in
the wilderness, letting God call me by name and
take me to a deeper place of the peace that the
world cannot give and can no longer take from one
once it is encountered."   —*St. Anthony Messenger*

crossroad